GARDENWARE

GARDENWARE

Martin Lungley

The Crowood Press

First published in 1999 by
The Crowood Press Ltd
Ramsbury, Marlborough
Wiltshire SN8 2HR

Acknowledgements
I give special thanks for the help and support
received from Ffion Meleri Davies, Shaun Roberts
and Peter Starkey.

British Library Cataloguing-in-Publication Data
A catalogue record for this book is available from the
British Library.

ISBN 1 86126 226 4

Photograph previous page: a large moulded urn.

Dedication
To J.B. and M.N.

Typefaces used: text and headings, ITC Giovanni;
chapter headings, ITC Tiepolo.

Typeset and designed by
D & N Publishing
Membury Business Park, Lambourn Woodlands
Hungerford, Berkshire.

Printed and bound by Times Offset, Malaysia.

Contents

1 History

Terracotta has been used by every civilization as a building material and for the production of pottery. Earliest artefacts were often in the form of figures and used for magical or religious purposes. Mother goddesses have been excavated in various parts of the world. They symbolize fertility and were used to encourage the birth of children and growth of crops. The first vessels made from clay were produced when communities became established in one area – nomadic tribes had no use for fragile pottery. These early pots would have been hand-built by a variety of techniques, and shells or gourds may have been used as simple press moulds.

The effect fire has on clay was discovered around 6500BC roughly in the area of modern Iraq where pots were baked in open fires or pits. This process chemically changes the clay into pottery rendering it permanent. The first kilns that separated pots from the firebox, were invented around 4500BC. In these, wares were not blackened, thus allowing the production of more colourful highly decorated ware. It was however, the development of the axle around 3500BC which led to the greatest revolution in pottery making. The potter's wheel allowed production to be increased from tens of pots per day to hundreds. The first wheel, although a distant relative of those we use today, works on the same basic principle. Energy created by circular motion is converted into vertical movement of clay. Heavy stone flywheels were used first, these would be spun with the hand or a stick creating sufficient momentum to keep it spinning for quite some time. The potter sits or crouches next to the wheel and throws the pot at arm's length. This type of wheel is still widely used throughout India today. The first major improvement was to add a vertical shaft and a separate wheel-head, a design that is commonly known as the continental wheel. It allows pots to be thrown in a much more comfortable sitting position. Continued rotation can be maintained by kicking the flywheel with the foot. A further refinement was made to the shaft in eighteenth-century England. By adding a double bend (crank) and a side arm kick-bar the wheel-head can be turned more easily and consistently. The Leach kickwheel is a typical example of this type.

The achievement of these early potters is indeed remarkable. Primitive societies, using unsophisticated equipment, were able to produce beautiful, highly crafted wares on a scale not seen today. This is perhaps epitomized by the Terracotta Army of Emperor Qin that was made during the third-century BC to protect the emperor in his afterlife, and is generally considered to be the eighth wonder of the world. It is estimated to consist of 7,500 life-size figures and 100 horse-drawn chariots. Although opinions vary, it is generally considered that they were produced by press-moulding with a team of elite craftsmen following to model on the beards and facial expressions. Qin, China's first emperor, was responsible for initiating many monumental feats, including the building of the

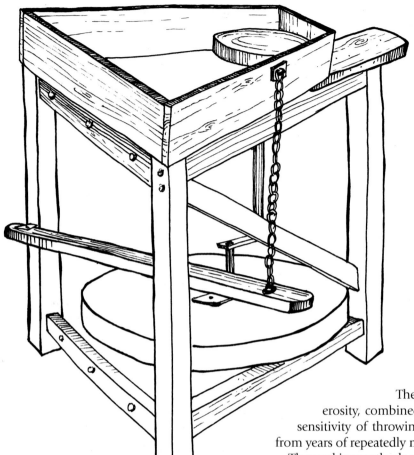

The Leach kickwheel.

'Great Wall' which he did by extending and linking previously smaller barriers to form a continuous line of defence stretching over three thousand kilometres.

Cretan Pottery

Large earthenware jars have been made for over three-thousand years in Crete. Originally they were used for the storage of oil, wine and cereals. The invention of plastic, which is durable, versatile and inexpensive, has changed their function. They are now marketed as exclusive, high-quality flowerpots and adorn many a stately home in this country and across Europe. The modern jars have changed little. The forms have a strength and generosity, combined with a beautiful freedom and sensitivity of throwing. This clay feeling only comes from years of repeatedly making the same forms.

The working methods and equipment too have changed little over the centuries. A team of six men known as a Vendema would produce the ware during the summer months (the rest of the year being devoted to agriculture). The men would arrive mid-May with production being completed by mid-September. Each man within the Vendema had a clearly defined task:

> the Master Potter
> the Second Potter
> the Wheeler
> the Clay Man
> the Wood Cutter
> the Carrier.

Fields are chosen that have the three essential materials: good sources of clay, water and wood for fuel. If the location has been used before then any necessary repairs to accommodation and kiln are completed before production begins. Clay preparation is done indoors, turntables (wheels) are set up outside in the sun so the jars can dry quickly.

Work generally begins at 4:30am. Clay brought in the day before is prepared, pounded, sieved and then kneaded with water ready for use. Plastic clay is not stored or left to sour, but always prepared immediately before it is required. Throwing begins around 6am and finishes around 5pm with between ten to sixteen jars being produced. The kiln is fired in four to five hours, starting early afternoon and finishing around sunset.

The Turntable

A long trench is dug that is widened at half-metre intervals by digging small square recesses known as 'hearths'; these house the wheels. The wheel-head itself is just above ground level with the wheeler sitting on the floor of the trench cross-legged rotating the wheel by pushing on arms that jut out of the vertical spindle. The spindle is made of olivewood that becomes smooth with friction and the wheel-head is made of plane wood.

Cretan pottery.

The Cretan turntable.

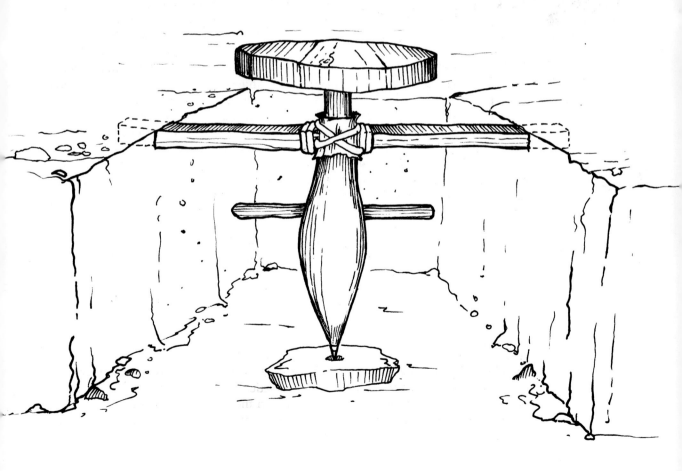

Making the Pots

The master potter sits on the trench opposite the wheeler and throws the base of the pot. This process is completed on each wheel-head along the trench by which time the first pot is dry enough to work on again. The remaining sections are added by throwing coils. The second potter squeezes out the coils vertically between his hands from approximately four to five kilograms of clay. Two or three are needed to complete each section. The master potter then throws these coils, each one taking about fifteen minutes to complete.

Drying

At the end of the day a whole row of pots stand completed on the turntables. They are left there until the next day when they are lifted off and placed behind the trench.

The Kiln

The Cretan kiln is of the updraught type and is really just an upright cylinder built of heavy stone walls. The largest kilns are up to three metres in diameter. The inside is lined with a clay and sand mixture. About a third of the way up a floor raises the pots above the fire; the top is open so loaded pots are covered with shards to hold the heat inside.

Firing

The firing is started slowly with just a few twigs being burnt at intervals. For the first hour the stoking gradually increases with cypress wood being burnt in bundles, and then finally whole bushes are thrown into the firebox. When the shards on top of the kiln turn white and the smoke has turned from black to thin and white the firing is complete. The kiln is unpacked the following morning at dawn by the master potter and the kiln man.

Slaking the Jars

The next day the jars are rinsed with water and the following day they are filled with water and left for at least one month. Gradually they become impermeable and suitable for storing oil.

Italian Renaissance Terracotta

The importance of this period for its influence on Terracotta production, architecture and its contribution to art in general is well-documented. Many of the forms, decoration and techniques in this book are inspired by those early Italian designs.

The mid-fifteenth century marked a revival in terracotta making in Tuscany. Many of the modern kiln sites around Sienna date from then. Luca Della Robbia was an instrumental figure. His workshop produced relief panels, free-standing terracotta figures and ornate terracotta pots that were exported all over Europe. In the village of Impruneta the tradition is still very much alive today with pots being both thrown and press-moulded from large plaster moulds. The clay is prepared by beating it to a fine powder and then mixing it with enough water to make it plastic.

Like the Cretans the Italians too produced large thrown jars for olive oil but their technique differed in that they assembled thrown sections rather than throwing coils. These sumptuous jars were often honey glazed and fired upside down resting on their rims. When the glaze became fluid in the kiln it ran and dripped off the pots leaving beautiful dribbles and streaks. When the jars are returned upright these glaze runs appear to be defying gravity and running skyward.

For very large pots or very ornate pots plaster moulds were used. Slabs or coils of clay are patted into the moulds, overlapped slightly so the joins can be properly worked together. The advantage of this technique is that any shape can be made whether it be square, rectangular or oblong. Many of the moulds presently used in the village of Impruneta were developed during the eighteenth and nineteenth centuries. The kilns used are mainly cross-draught and up to five metres in length, traditionally fired with wood gathered from the Tuscan hills, but now they are generally fired with oil or propane.

Italian Renaissance terracotta.

English Country Pottery

Interest in gardening grew steadily from the seventeenth century onwards, creating a new demand for containers of all shapes and sizes. These containers were used mainly for propagation and as a way of transporting plants easily. By the mid-nineteenth century the country pottery was in its heyday, a nurseryman could choose from a selection of flowerpots unparalleled anywhere in the world. Large nurseries would often place orders in the region of half a million pots annually. Every size and shape of plant was catered for. The range included full pots, half pots, seed pans and longtoms, in a staggering array of sizes together with forcing pots, strawberry pots and other specialized items.

English country pottery.

Pots were made in batches known as 'casts' – a unit of clay which weighed half a hundredweight (approximately 25kg). A potter would be expected to throw twenty casts a day regardless of the size of pot being made. A pot that weighed a full cast was a number one, with the smallest being a number ninety, meaning ninety pots to make a full cast.

The First World War was responsible for the closure of many country potteries. A large number of the young men never returned, and those who did went into better paid jobs. The Second World War accounted for yet more and with the closure of Soil Hill pottery in the 1960s and the death of Reg Harris of Wrecclesham Pottery in 1983 many thought the era of the country pottery had come to a close. The pots they produced had a quality and an honesty about them that is seldom seen today. They may only have been quickly thrown, inexpensive and often rough, but they exude true craftsmanship and an affinity with, and an enjoyment of, the material that only comes with repeated making.

There are, however, potteries keeping these traditions alive. Among them are Whichford pottery, Willow pottery and S & B Evans and Sons, who are making high-quality gardenware in the time-honoured way.

2 Clay and its Preparation

Clays vary enormously in terms of shrinkage, strength, colour and plasticity. In order to save time from fruitless experiments and testing it is very helpful to have some understanding of the material with which we work. Clay decomposes from feldspar, which in turn has decomposed from igneous rock. It has a tiny crystal structure, which is too small for the eye to see. These groups of crystals form particles, which are flat and plate-like and roughly hexagonal in shape. Water lubricates them as it would between sheets of glass, allowing them to slide over one another and an electrical attraction and gravity maintain cohesion. Plasticity is a property some clays have to withstand vigorous handling during forming. The particle size and shape of the clay has a direct bearing on its plasticity. Clays with small particles and water content in the region of 40 per cent, by weight are generally very plastic. The water content is divided into three categories and is made up of 20 per cent lubricant, 10 per cent to fill the pores and a further 10 per cent that is chemically combined with the clay particles.

Water of Plasticity
The lubricant that enables the particles to slide over each other.

Pore Water
Water that is locked inside the pores of dry clay. As clay dries it is imprisoned by the surrounding particles. It can account for as much as 10 per cent of the weight of apparently dry clay. It is only driven off when the clay is heated above 100°C. For this reason the early stage of a firing is always taken slowly to avoid pore water expanding rapidly when turning to steam. This stage of the firing is called 'steaming' or the 'water smoking' period.

Chemically Combined Water
Sometimes known as bound water. This is part of the clay's chemical structure. This water is driven off in the firing between 450–700°C. The risk of pots

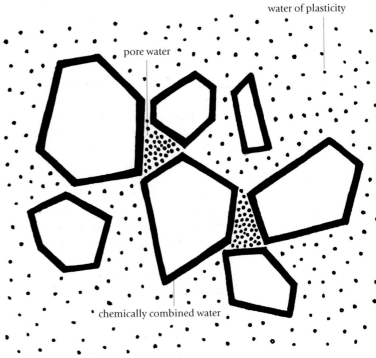

Water content of clay.

water of plasticity

pore water

chemically combined water

13

exploding is small. When this process is completed an irreversible change has taken place, turning clay into pottery.

Primary Clay

Clay can be easily divided into two main groups, primary and secondary clays. Clays that occur in their place of origin are primary clays. They tend to be very pure (white), have a large particle size and are generally low in plasticity. The most common example is China clay, so called because deposits were used in China as much as 1200 years before their discovery in Europe. China clay is also known as Kaolin derived from the word 'Kao-ling' meaning high ridge, possibly the first area in China where it was found. China clay is the purest of natural clays. It has many uses, in bodies it is used for whiteness, to clarify colour (particularly in the case of commercially prepared red clays) and to control vitrification. It is also an important ingredient in porcelain and bone china. In glazes it is used to add alumina. This helps to stiffen the glaze and stop it running off the pot. China clay is very refractory, vitrifying by 1770°C, so it is of great value when producing kilns and furnaces.

Secondary Clay

The second group is composed of clays that have been transported from their original site by water or ice and are known as secondary clays, or sedimentary clays. This category covers most clays. They have a finer particle size due to the constant milling received in transit. They vary in colour and texture, most secondary clays pick up iron and free silica. The iron gives grey, cream, orange, red or brown colours after firing. Free silica is sometimes in the form of quartz sand with grains big enough to be seen with the naked eye. This helps to provide excellent 'bite' or 'tooth' giving a superb, strong throwing body. They may also have picked up organic matter, which can give the raw clay a darker colour and have an unpleasant odour, however this burns out when the pots reach red heat.

Secondary clays include red clays, fire clays, stoneware clays and ball clays. The term Ball Clay originates from the seventeenth century when for ease of handling in transit from Devonshire to Stoke-on-Trent it was made into balls. As a general rule secondary clays are more plastic and fuse at a lower temperature than primary clays.

Red Clay

As it is the production of gardenware that concerns us, red clay or Terracotta is of greatest interest. The term Terracotta simply means fired earth. Although not strictly precise, it is often used to describe earthenware clays that burn red due to their iron content. Some red clays will contain as much as 8 per cent iron but even 2 per cent will give a strong colour. The most recent deposits may date back less than a million years but these are probably re-deposits from up to 500-million-year-old seams.

Red earthenware clays vary in colour when dug so they are subdivided into the following groups. Dark or blackish clays are often known as Grey or Terracotta clay. Yellow or greenish-yellow clays are called Ochres. Some red clays, notably from Stoke-on-Trent, are called Marls although this is not completely accurate. A Marl by definition is a pink burning clay in which calcium has had a bleaching effect on the iron content.

The Etruria marl on which Stoke-on-Trent's pottery industry is established is the most commonly available commercial red clay. It has a larger particle size than many local red clay deposits and is generally less plastic than most. Therefore an Etruria marl may seem less pleasant to work with and generally may be less suitable than a local clay in terms of the following:

Workability. Pots may sag while being thrown, or have to be made from hard clay, which can slow down production and may eventually result in wrist and back problems. Large amounts of grog may have to be added making pots fragile when raw.

Cost. Etruria marls mature at around 1150°C while many local clays can be fired to around 1000°C to make them frost-proof, this saving on the fuel bill could be considerable. The clay too may be as much as a quarter of the price from a local brickyard.

Character. Commercial clays are highly refined smooth bodies. Many local clays are not so refined and retain some shale or quartz sand giving them a more interesting 'organic' quality that is somehow more in keeping with both traditional flowerpots and the garden environment.

Having said this, if you are in the business of making gardenware for a living, then commercial clays based on an Etruria marl have two outstanding virtues. Firstly they are ready prepared. Just by making a simple phone call, five tonnes of plastic clay can miraculously appear outside the workshop. For small pots it can sometimes be thrown from the bag without any preparation. Generally, though, a quick cut wedging or kneading is required to prepare the body for throwing. There is no need for the blunging, sieving, filter pressing, pugging and souring which brickyard clay may require. Secondly, it is very consistent and reliable. You know what you are getting so you can develop a method of working to suit that body – this is very important particularly when orders have to be fulfilled and deadlines are approaching. When using brickyard clay, problems may suddenly arise such as lime contamination or scumming because clay has been supplied from a different part of the quarry. This can result in kiln loads of pots being ruined.

Ultimately the choice of which clay to use is a very personal thing. For me a commercial clay is best. I work largely alone and use around twenty tonnes of clay per year. I feel my time is better spent on production than preparation. Commercial clays may not be as plastic but you definitely develop a technique or style of throwing to overcome this. A range of work can also be developed that suits a smoother clay. This may mean more detailed or ornate decoration. As a general rule the larger the scale of your production the greater the opportunity is for financial saving and the more appealing preparing your own body may seem. When deciding which is more appropriate for you, consider the following points:

Size of your workshop. For the average size workshop preparing a local clay may take up as much as half your working area.

Size of production and work force. The amount of time spent preparing a local body may equal the throwing time. It may be necessary to recruit extra labour so time is not lost from production.

Capital investments. Machinery such as blungers, dough mixers, pugmills and filter presses may be required to prepare the clay quickly and efficiently. These should be available second-hand from suppliers in Stoke, but this will still require significant investment.

Location. If you are situated near to a good source of red clay this will dramatically reduce otherwise expensive haulage costs.

Ultimately when all is said and done, it will probably be a question of economics. Will money saved on cheaper firings and reduced clay bills cover the expense of buying and running the necessary equipment and extra labour costs?

Clay Preparation

Thorough preparation of clay is a necessity and for throwing it is essential. In many ways it is the potter's most important activity; very often problems that arise during production can be traced back to the choice of clay or its preparation. Sometimes these problems can go undetected until pots have been fired, occasionally resulting in whole firings being unsellable. The pitfalls are many. Inappropriate choice of clay, addition of the wrong type or quantity of grog, poorly wedged or the wrong consistency of clay, scumming and lime contamination can all have disastrous effects. Experience is the best solution, getting to know your material and range of work through repetition. However, with the aid of some practical advice hopefully this section will help you avoid some of the problems.

Testing a Local Clay

Brickyards and tile manufacturers often mark the existence of a good deposit of red clay. It will need testing though to assess its suitability for pot making. Small quantities can be prepared for this purpose quite simply. If possible collect approximately half a dustbin full of clay, break it up into pebble-sized pieces then let it dry thoroughly. Soak it with water and leave it until all of the hard lumps have disintegrated, dry clay breaks down very quickly and should not take more than a day or two. The slurry can be placed on plaster bats or in material-lined boxes to de-water. When it has dried to a plastic consistency it can be pugged or hand-wedged and thrown to test for workability (plasticity). A clay low in plasticity may benefit from being aged or soured for a period of time. If it appears 'flabby' (lacks strength and sags easily) it may be improved by the addition of sand, grog or a mixture of both in quantities up to 30 per cent.

Pots can then be fired to test for shrinkage, firing range, colour, lime content and scumming. Shrinkage can be most accurately tested for by producing a series of test tiles of a known length – 10cm is a convenient size – then fired to a range of temperatures between 1000°C and 1200°C. They are then re-measured to calculate the shrinkage. This will also give an indication of the fired colour and firing range.

Shrinkage in the region of 10 per cent to 12 per cent is acceptable. If it is greater than 13 per cent or 14 per cent you may consider adding sand or grog to counteract any warping or cracking, this often occurs in clays that shrink excessively during drying and firing.

Some surface clays have soluble salts present that can form an unpleasant white scum on fired pots. This can be prevented by the addition of barium carbonate in amounts of up to 2 per cent (dry weight). This will fix the salts and give the pots a clean bright appearance.

Lime is a common impurity and can cause severe disruption to production. It sometimes goes undetected until weeks after firing. It expands as it sucks moisture through the pot wall and eventually bursts its way out. Lime can be removed by sieving the clay while it is still a slurry through a 40-mesh sieve.

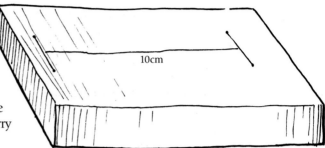

10cm

Tile for testing shrinkage.

Preparing a Local Clay

If the Gods are smiling on you, maybe you're fortunate enough to have a good source of red clay locally. If it is clean of roots, stones, lime, is inexpensive, highly plastic and most importantly in plentiful supply, fantastic! Roll up your sleeves and start throwing. For other clays some preparation will be necessary. Some will have all of the above attributes except plasticity. This could be due to a high proportion of shale or quartz sand being present. If this is the case the addition of a smooth throwing body such as an Etruria Marl may be all that's required. Anywhere between 10 per cent and 70 per cent can be added to achieve the desired effect. Ball clays can also be added in similar proportions, but due to their low iron content they will have a bleaching effect on the colour of the fired clay. These can be wedged in by hand or preferably pugged in. They may need to be pugged twice and a de-airing pug will give a denser more workable body. Bentonite and Fuller's Earth can be added in quantities of up to 5 per cent to increase plasticity, they are super-plastic stoneware clays and consequently are best blunged into a body. Local clays can also be purchased in a dry granular form. There are two ways in which this can be made into a plastic consistency, the dry or the slop methods.

Dry Mixing

This is a very simple low-tech method of preparing clay. Spread out the granules on a concrete base or a purpose-made shallow tank about 9in (23cm) deep. Spray them with water until puddles start to form, a fairly fine jet from a hosepipe is best. The next day turn the clay with a spade and spray on more water if necessary. The following day the clay should be ready to pug. If the clay is 'short' it may need to be left to 'rest' for a few days. If this does not improve the plasticity sufficiently then the clay may need to 'age' or 'sour' for a period of time, between one and three months is usual. The clay will then have to be repugged before throwing. Quantities of half a ton or more can be efficiently prepared by this method. This procedure can be mechanized by using a dough mixer, which can be bought cheaply second-hand. They generally require a three-phase electricity supply though, and that can be costly to install.

Slop Mixing

This method involves mixing the clay with sufficient water to turn it into a liquid, then drying it out to a plastic consistency. The advantage of this over dry mixing is that clay particles are able to absorb more water, allowing them to divide more easily. Therefore clays that are not plastic when prepared by dry mixing may be improved by preparing them by this method instead. If a clay contains roots, stones or lime it will also have to be made into a slurry, then sieved to extract the unwanted materials. Clay granules can be mixed with water quite well by hand, but this task is most easily performed with the aid of a blunger. Ten minutes high-speed blunging is said to have the same effect on a clay body as a whole winter's weathering. A blunger is a large mixing tank and one that contains approximately 300 gallons (1,360 litres) is necessary to prepare clay bodies for plant pot production. Inside blades rotate blending the clay and water into a fine slip. If necessary the slip can be sieved to remove unwanted materials. A 30- or 40-mesh sieve is adequate, a finer one will extract the 'tooth' from the clay. Three methods of drying clay to a plastic consistency are described, however without the aid of mechanization some foresight and patience are needed.

Firstly, the slurry can be placed outdoors in wooden troughs and left to dry slowly. When the clay dries to a plastic consistency it can be removed and pugged. As a guide, this may take up to two months. This will obviously vary with the seasons and a prolonged windy spell will reduce this time considerably. The troughs, that I first saw used by David Frith in the late 1980s can be made from modified forklift pallets and should be lined with rot-proof filter press cloth. They are held in position by fixing them onto 4in ¥ 2in (10cm ¥ 5cm) planks and if necessary can then be mounted onto concrete piers to give extra height. The top can be covered with weatherproofed boards or PVC. The troughs should be filled with clay to a depth of approximately 4in (10cm), they should not be filled more than about 6in (15cm) or the clay will not dry evenly. To ensure production does not stop if there is a prolonged damp spell, construct the troughs so they can contain more clay than you can use in ten weeks.

*T*rough for drying clay.

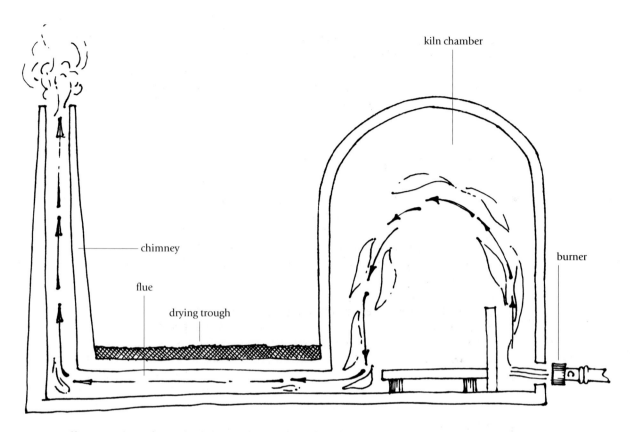

kiln chamber

chimney

flue

drying trough

burner

Secondly, waste heat from the kiln can be used. Soil Hill pottery, an old country pottery near Halifax (now closed), used this method to dry their clay. The kiln's exit flues are elongated. The area above can be made into a drying trough to contain the slurry. When the kiln is fired it should provide sufficient heat to dry the clay to a plastic consistency. To maintain continuity of production the trough must contain enough clay to throw a minimum of one and a half kiln loads of pots.

*D*rying clay using a kiln's waste heat.

Thirdly, if your money is burning a hole in your pocket you may wish to invest in an Ark and Filter press. This is the way industry prepares plastic bodies and it is by far the most efficient method. After being sieved, clay is run off or pumped into an Ark. This is a large storage tank in which slip is stirred to prevent it from settling. From here it is pumped into the filter press. This is a series of cast iron 'leaves' that traps the clay. After a few hours of pumping slip, water is squeezed out and cakes of plastic clay are formed. It is then pugged, some clays being ready for immediate use and some needing to be aged and repugged.

Grog

Grog is fired clay that has been ground into a grit or dust. Fire clay, because of its refractory properties is often used. Grog is graded according to its size and given a number relating to the mesh size it will fit through. For example, 40-mesh indicates forty holes per square inch. A 40/60 grade means all the grog can pass through a 40-mesh but not all can pass through a 60-mesh sieve. Forty/Dust means the grog is a mixture of sizes from 40-mesh with the smallest particles being very fine indeed. Sand also comes into this category and builder's soft sand is a useful addition to an earthenware body. Grog can be classified as either hard or soft. Hard grogs are those that have been previously fired to a higher temperature than the body will be fired to. They are used to reduce shrinkage, warping and cracking during drying and firing. Soft grogs are those which have been fired to a lower temperature than the body will be fired to, sometimes as low as 800°C. If the soft grog is made of the same clay as the body it is called pitchers. Their main advantage is that they will not alter the fired character of the clay. Soft grogs make a useful additive when a clay is low in workable strength or excessively sticky. They will be of some help in reducing shrinkage and because of their porous nature, aid the drying of ware.

Sand is the cheapest and most commonly used additive to red clay. When preparing a body for throwing plant pots, up to 30 per cent sand can be added to give extra workable strength and reduce shrinkage. This can be blunged in or pugged into the body. Alternatively it can be bought directly from potter merchants who supply red clays that contain 10 per cent or 20 per cent sand. When producing press-moulded ware, or particularly large or thick ware, a coarser grog may be more suitable. One such as Eight/Dust will open the body and the variety in particle size will create a stronger matrix resulting in a stronger body.

As a general rule, the addition of sand or grog will reduce shrinkage, control, warping and improve a clay's workable strength. However it is worth noting that some highly plastic clays that are prone to cracking during drying may benefit as much from the addition of a clay low in plasticity.

Lime Contamination

Lime contamination is of particular nuisance to the potter. It often occurs in the form of a chalk seam running through clay beds or as fossils scattered arbitrarily through a deposit. It very often goes unnoticed during making and is sometimes only detected days or even weeks after firing. As the pot absorbs moisture the lime expands forcing off a large chunk from the wall or rim of the pot. The crater this leaves will have a telltale white speck of lime at its centre.

The addition of common salt to a clay body is said to help prevent lime blows, but the most effective way is to make the clay into a slurry and extract all impurities through a 40-mesh sieve. If lime is suspected it can be tested for in raw clay by placing a small piece in a dilute hydrochloric acid; if the clay fizzes and bubbles lime is present. It may be easier to test for by soaking any suspect fired pots in water – lime will soon burst its way out if present.

Scumming

Some surface clays have soluble salts present that do not appear in the raw state but form an unpleasant white scum on fired pots. Where the pot has been handled fingerprints will turn white and rims or edges seem particularly susceptible to scumming.

It can be prevented by the addition of barium carbonate to the clay in an amount between 0.25 per cent and 2 per cent. This should be mixed in at the slurry stage and blunging is the preferred method.
(N.B. Barium is a toxic material and should be treated with care.)

Improving a Clay's Plasticity

Short

A short clay is one which has little plasticity or strength. It shows signs of tearing or cracking when curved and has insufficient workability for most tasks set upon it. The clay can either be naturally short in which case plastic clay such as a ball clay can be added to it. Or the clay's strength has been destroyed due to overworking on the wheel or pugmill. In this case the colloidal attraction between the fine particles is lost resulting in tired weak clay. Plasticity can be improved by the following methods.

Ageing

Ageing is the storage of soft plastic clay to improve its workability (plasticity). It is a physical action where water slowly penetrates between particles producing an increased number of particles of a smaller size. This water penetration results in the clay hardening, therefore it should be stored in a softer state than required for throwing. During the ageing process clay is also compressed under its own weight, that brings particles closer together making the clay stronger and more workable. This action can be simulated by pugging (through a de-airing pugmill) which is said to be equivalent to two months' natural ageing.

Souring

This is a bacteriological process that involves leaving the clay for a period of time in damp storage. Organic material naturally present in clay breaks down resulting in the release of carbon and temporary discoloration. The bacteria present within the organic material use oxygen to multiply which produces amino acids. These acids alter the physical properties of the fine clay particles, forming a 'colloidal gel' resulting in improved strength. This process can take something between one and three months depending on the amount of bacteria present. However the introduction of a small amount of very sour clay can speed up the process. Wine, cider or a gardener's soil disinfectant can also be added in small amounts to the clay to encourage bacterial growth and souring.

Weathering

This is the process responsible for the erosion and transposition of clay from the parent rock. Through the action of rain, wind and frost, clay particles divide into a network of smaller particles thus increasing plasticity. Weathering is traditionally used by country potteries where potting was seasonal. Clay would be dug in the autumn and prepared into a plastic body in the spring after the last frosts. The improvement that weathering may have on a very short clay in one winter is limited. Even so it may well be enough to produce a workable body.

Pugmill

This is the machine used for mixing and compressing a plastic body thoroughly. Clay is forced through a tapered barrel, inside which blades rotate where the clay is minced and shredded. A de-airing pugmill works in the same way but usually has two barrels, separated by a vacuum chamber. This sucks the air from the clay bringing particles into closer contact making a denser more workable body. Pugmills are very useful when preparing large quantities of clay or when adding sand/grog or mixing different plastic bodies together. Clay is extruded in the form of a long sausage so 'sticks' can be cut in a variety of lengths to measure out each different weight of clay you use. Simply mark and cut as clay is extruded from the pugmill. This saves much of the time otherwise spent on weighing out or 'balling up' clay on scales by hand.

Wedging

Whether the source of your clay is a potter's merchant or a local clay pit, once plastic it should need only rudimentary preparation before throwing. If the clay is freshly pugged it may be of a sufficiently even consistency to be thrown without any further preparation. If clay is stored for any length of time, water within the body migrates often making the outside sticky. If this is the case wedging or repugging is necessary to regain a homogeneous consistency. If you do not have access to a pugmill you will have to prepare clay by cut wedging and kneading. Wedging is preferred for preparing reclaim clay, mixing two different clay bodies together and introducing sand or grog into a body. It is a process where clay is continually cut in half with a wire then slammed together. A strong bench is necessary, a slab of slate or marble is considered best for the top although a paving slab placed onto concrete block piers makes a very good cheap alternative.

*T*he clay is cut in half with a wire.

*O*ne half is slammed on top of the other (above left).

*C*utting the clay a second time (above).

*C*utting and slamming the two pieces together continues (left).

Drop and beat the clay into an oblong-shaped lump. Drop the clay at a slope with the furthest end resting on the bench and the nearest end raised slightly. Place a strong wire under the clay and cut vertically upwards through the middle creating two equal sized pieces. Examine each piece for unwanted material such as hard lumps, stones or plastic. Pick up the half nearest you in both hands to head height, then slam it down on top of the other piece to form two layers with both cut edges facing you.

The whole piece is rolled towards you and turned over. (So the bottom now becomes the top). Roll the clay backwards and forward gently to return the piece to its original

Further cuts and slamming together are performed.

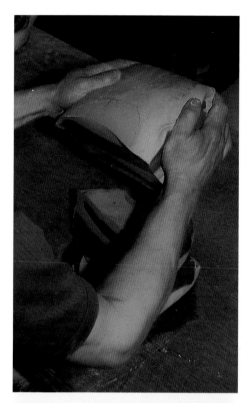

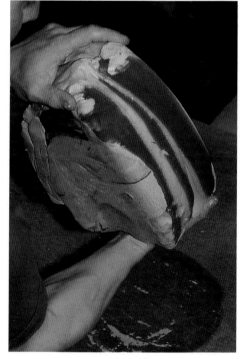

shape. When this is achieved pick the lump up and turn it 45 degrees in a clockwise direction. Drop the clay at a slope as at the first stage, with the front end raised to return to the starting position ready for the next cut. This process is repeated 20–25 times, forming over one million layers.

*H*ere the clay is mixing together well. After 20–25 cuts, the clay will mix completely.

*S*piral kneading (below).

If sand or grog is to be wedged into the clay it is best to mix it with a slurry first. The lump of clay is then cut into two layers and the grog slurry sandwiched between. The standard wedging method is now followed, however it may take more than 20–25 cuts to be mixed in thoroughly.

Kneading

The final preparation is kneading which mixes the clay thoroughly and expels any air bubbles. It is often done to a piece of clay that is weighed out exactly for repetition throwing. Spiral kneading is an oriental technique where the clay is repeatedly folded over on itself to form a shell-like pattern. The clay is patted into an oblong shape. With hands cupped behind the clay, push down and slightly leftwards to produce a fold in the clay with the heel of the right hand. The top of the clay is then rolled back up and

Forming these folds mixes clay thoroughly.

round a quarter-turn in a clockwise direction. These two processes are rhythmically repeated until many folds have been produced and the clay feels smooth, even, and all air bubbles are expelled.

The clay is rolled to form a cone shape (right).

The clay is flattened into a ball ready for throwing (far right).

3 Throwing

For studio potteries and small workshops throwing is still the most common and convenient method used for production. A skilled potter can throw as much as half a tonne of clay in one day which can amount to several hundred pots. A whole array of wares can be produced of various shapes and sizes and with many different styles of decoration. There is no need for bulky plaster moulds and expensive equipment – the potter's wheel is the only sizeable investment and even this can be bought cheaply second-hand or can even be homemade.

Throwing is a process that is only really mastered through constant repetition. The basic techniques can be taught, but a feel for the material only comes with lots of experience. An apprenticeship of seven years was considered necessary to learn to throw in the old country potteries. To the student who has worked hard at their technique for say a year or more this may seem somewhat bewildering, for by this time they may have enough skill to make quite large pots. However I can testify from personal experience that this passage of time brings an increased feeling of control and confidence. Indeed a skilled thrower in the middle of a production run, when hand, eye, material, and machine are in harmony will often have a tremendous feeling of oneness with the process.

Until the advent of the First World War there were many country potteries employing hundreds of throwers. Throwing

was considered a trade; it involves the acquiring of a set of techniques rather than the appreciation of form and aesthetics. So like other trades most people have the facility or are naturally well co-ordinated enough to learn it. The most important attribute that a would-be thrower needs is enthusiasm – the ability to take the setbacks and disappointments that will inevitably come when learning and not be too disheartened. Perseverance brings great reward and there is tremendous satisfaction to be had from surveying a whole rack of freshly thrown pots at the end of a hard day, content in the knowledge that everything created is the product of your own labour.

A distinction should be made between a thrower and a potter. As mentioned earlier a thrower is really only concerned with learning the set of skills that are required to throw a pot. Whereas a potter needs a much fuller understanding of the whole process, from clay preparation to making, drying, glazing and firing. Just to know the techniques is not enough, the potter must have the ability to marry together choice of clay, form and glaze in an intelligent, informed and considered way and to produce work that is individual and reflects something of the character of the maker.

H and positions on a pot compared to a clockface.

General Throwing Techniques

Various techniques can be used to centre, open out, lift and shape clay into a pot, many of which are equally effective. The tendency seems to be to stick to the first one you are taught or the first one you become comfortable with. The following descriptions are of techniques I use. If you throw already and these descriptions differ from the techniques you use, don't panic as your method may work just as well.

It is worth noting that for complete beginners written descriptions are a poor substitute for personal tuition that can be tailored to individual requirements. However I have tried to include as much detail as possible and cover all the common mistakes beginners tend to make.

It is important to note accurately which part of the pot the hands need to work on when throwing. To enable me to be quite specific I have chosen to compare the hand positions employed with the numbers on a clock face. With the nearest part of the wheel-head directly in front of you when sitting on the wheel being '6 o'clock' and the top edge of the wheel-head furthest away being '12 o'clock'. '3 o'clock' will naturally be on the right-hand side with '9 o'clock' being opposite on the left-hand side. Most of the centring is done with the hands in the left-hand quarter between '9–6 o'clock' with most of the lifting and shaping being completed with the hands on the right side between '4–6 o'clock'.

Centring

The objective is a simple one, to position the clay on the wheel-head so that it's even and centralized (not wobbling) when spinning. Irregular shaped or off-centre pots are generally caused by incorrect centring or badly prepared clay. Life is made much easier if you knead the clay just prior to throwing and make it into a ball or cone shape so less effort is needed to centre it. Before throwing commences the wheel-head should be slightly dampened so the clay will stick, but not wetted which may cause the clay to skid around when pressure is applied. The ball of clay is then placed on the stationary wheel-head and patted to get it as close to the centre as possible. Wheel-heads generally have concentric circles marked on them to aid positioning. Both clay and hands are now wetted and centring can begin. With the wheel-head spinning fast, steady pressure is applied with the palm of the left hand on the left side of the clay at '9 o'clock' and the fleshy part of the palm of the right hand on the top of the clay.

The hands are interlocked to give a steady firmness to control the clay. The left elbow can be tucked into the left ribs and both forearms can be rested on the wheel tray to give extra stability. Water is continually used for lubrication whenever the clay starts to stick to your hands. When centring, the top should be kept slightly domed so that the clay can be 'coned' more easily. Coning is a process used to push any unevenness in the clay up and out of the top; it also creates a spiral alignment of the particles, which gives added strength to the finished pot. The clay is squeezed between both palms up into a tall cone (the left hand at '9 o'clock' and the right at '3 o'clock'). It is then pushed back down with the hands in the conventional centring position, the clay

*P*atting the clay to position it as close to the centre as possible.

*T*he hands are interlocked to centre the clay.

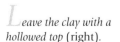

Coning up the clay (above).

Coning down the clay (above right).

becoming proportionally as wide as it is high. Coning can be repeated several times, maybe four or five, although if the clay has been very well wedged first one or two might be sufficient. When the clay is running smoothly and evenly between the hands you are ready to go on to the next stage. An important point to remember when centring is to concentrate on what your hands are supposed to be doing rather than what the clay is doing. It is common to see beginners watching the unevenness or 'swing' in an uncentred piece of clay and merely following it with their hands. If you keep your hands still then the clay too will become centred. When the clay is properly centred the top should be hollowed slightly so the fingers can be inserted for opening the clay out.

Leave the clay with a hollowed top (right).

Opening the Clay Out

Once centring is complete the fingers can be inserted to open the clay out. As the term suggests this is where an opening is made in the centred piece of clay and the base of the pot is formed. There is a difference when opening clay for gardenware as opposed to domestic ware; when producing gardenware the base of the pot and the drainage hole are made simultaneously. The clay should be centred so the top has a slight hollow; this will allow the fingers to find the centre of the clay quite easily. With the wheel still spinning fast the fingers of the left hand are placed onto the centre of the clay (in front of you at '6 o'clock'). The right hand is placed on top of the left hand to add support. The elbows should be lowered to rest on the wheel tray for extra stability. The fingers of the left hand are kept straight but bend at the knuckles to push down into the clay to open it out. The fingers penetrate through the clay to the wheel head; this forms the drainage hole. For small pots up to 10lb (4.5kg) a drainage hole slightly larger than a finger's width is sufficient. For large pots of 30lb (13.5kg) and over, a drainage hole of 1.5in (3.5cm) may be necessary and for pots with wide bases it is often a good idea to have more than one drainage hole.

Once the drainage hole is made and finished off neatly the base of the pot can be worked on, with the hands kept in the same position but the wheel spinning slightly slower. The wall of the pot is dragged directly towards you to a width slightly greater than that desired for the finished pot. It is important to try to keep the thickness of the base constant while this is being completed. If the base becomes thicker further from the centre of

The fingers are placed on the centre and pushed down.

Make a small hole in the bottom of the pot to form the drainage hole.

*P*ull the clay towards you to form the base.

*P*ush the clay up to form a conical shape (right).

the pot, clay is wasted and the pot will be too heavy. Alternatively, if the base becomes thinner further from the centre this will result in a weakness in the base and greater risk of cracking. As a guide, pots of 10lb (4.5kg) and under will need a base 0.5cm thick and for large pots of 30lb (13.5kg) and over a base of 1cm will be necessary. The base of the pot is then compressed with a crooked index finger. This finishes off the base neatly and helps to make it an even thickness. Compressing the base will also reduce many of the 's' shaped cracks that unfortunately occur during drying and firing.

With the base of the pot finished the wall can be worked on. The aim is to make the pot the shape of a truncated cone; that is to say, the top of the pot is

made narrower than the bottom. This is important; centrifugal force acts upon the clay as it revolves resulting in the pot naturally becoming wider. For this reason pots are kept narrow until the full height is achieved. It is much easier to widen a pot if it is too narrow than it is to make it narrower if it becomes too wide. This is achieved by placing the heel of the left hand against the bottom of the pot directly in front of you at '6 o'clock'; the fingers are cupped over the rim. The right hand is again placed on top of the left to add support. The hands are pushed in and upwards to the rim – this results in the top narrowing and the height of the pot increasing. This should also have the effect of producing a sharp corner on the inside where the base meets the wall. This will allow the wall of the pot to be lifted without leaving a mass of clay at the bottom. Sometimes narrowing the top will make it uneven (particularly if the clay was not centred properly or was insufficiently well wedged). This can be corrected by supporting the rim between the thumb and index finger of the left hand and applying downward pressure with the right index finger. Alternatively the left hand can be placed on the left-hand side of the pot for support. Downward pressure is applied on the right-hand side of the pot by the webbed part between the middle and ring fingers of the right hand the fingers straddling the rim. To control the pot, slight inward pressure should be applied which also has the effect of making the pot narrower and is sometimes referred to as collaring. Once the top is levelled the pot is ready for the next stage – lifting.

Lifting the Walls of the Pot

A professional potter normally requires only three lifts to make a pot its full height, working quickly and efficiently to leave the pot looking fresh and crisp when finished. The secret lies in understanding and mastering the relationship between three important factors.

Collar the top to keep it even.

- How fast the wheel needs to spin
- How firmly to squeeze the clay
- How quickly to lift the clay with the fingers

If a harmonious balance is achieved between these three forces (spinning, squeezing and lifting) then the pot will rise effortlessly, like magic. A real understanding and feel for the material is necessary to fashion the clay in this manner and this is only gained through constant repetition. To begin with six or more lifts may be necessary. Lifting is performed by applying pressure to the wall of the pot. With the left hand on the inside and the right hand on the outside, for most people the hands work at about '5 o'clock'. The one exception to this is when very large pots are being thrown and the hand position can move round to '8 o'clock' for the first lift, with the right hand on the inside and the left on the outside. For pots up to 2lb (900g) the fingertips of both hands are used to lift the wall of the pot. For pots larger than 2lb the fingertips of the left hand are used on the inside and the knuckles of the right hand on the outside.

When lifting, the speed of the wheel-head is crucial – it needs to be slowed considerably to a modest level so control over the pot is maintained. Starting at the bottom with

*T*he first lift.

*T*he rim is flattened and given its final shape.

*F*orming a 'roll' of clay to gain height.

*S*tarting to shape the pot.

the hands positioned at about '4 o'clock' the clay is squeezed to produce a thinning in the wall of the pot. This position is held for several seconds to ensure that the thinning is consistent all the way round. Creating this thinning in the wall results in a thickening forming immediately above, what potters call a 'roll' of clay. The aim is to lift this roll up to the rim of the pot in one fairly slow continuous movement like a wave rolling onto a seashore. When the rim of the pot is reached it is held for a few seconds and then gently released. It is important not to release too quickly otherwise the wall of the pot may spring off centre. Be sure to apply enough water first to ensure that your hands do not stick to the clay during the course of a lift. If necessary, the pot can be collared and the rim straightened after each lift, as described earlier in opening the clay out. Rims on plant pots are generally fairly heavy in order to give the pot a generously satisfying conclusion and to make it less susceptible to chipping. To produce this type of rim, it is important to thicken it after each lift to a heaviness greater than that required for the final shape. When the pot is widened to form the final shape, the rim will automatically become thinner. I often take this one stage further and give the rim its final shape after the first lift and make any further corrections necessary to keep it that shape after each subsequent lift. This has two advantages. Firstly it is often difficult and time consuming to shape a rim on a pot when it is soft and thin, near completion. Secondly if a pot goes slightly off-centre when shaping it is quite awkward to shape the rim and often the pot will be made more off-centre by trying to. Lifting is completed three times, with the second lift differing from the first

Using a wooden rib during shaping.

only in that the diameter of the rim is widened so that the pot forms the shape of a cooling tower. This is particularly necessary when making wide-rimmed pots. The third lift is used to bring any spare clay left up from the bottom. The objective is to make the wall of the pot the same thickness at the top as at the bottom. It is also often used to start the shaping process.

Shaping the Pot

Shaping, even on large pots is a delicate process. Manipulating the clay when it is soft and thin takes great care so the fingertips of both hands are generally used for greater sensitivity. On short, bulbous or wide forms shaping can be started on the third lift. For taller straighter shapes it is often done separately after the full height of the cylinder is reached. The fingertips gently caress the wall of the pot pushing out from the inside with the left hand to make the pot wider, or in from the outside with the right hand to make it narrower. The hands are positioned at about '4 o'clock' (the same as for lifting) and just guide the wall into the right shape. The walls will automatically become thinner if the pot is widened so it is important not to squeeze the clay as in lifting and to leave the wall slightly thicker if wide-bellied pots are being made. Wooden ribs can also be used to shape a pot – the advantage they have over the fingertips is that they cover a greater area and thus give greater control. They also smooth the wall and take off throwing lines and slurry to give the pot a neater, more finished appearance.

Throwing Large Ware

The principles are the same whether throwing large or small pieces of clay. Centring, opening, lifting and shaping still have to be completed, but in practice a different set of techniques are best employed when throwing pieces around 15lb(7kg) and over. Making large pots is hard work and centring in particular is physically very demanding. Repeat throwing of big ware with a poor technique or clay that is too hard, puts undue pressure on joints and wrists in particular. To avoid exhaustion and injury it is necessary to get the clay close to the centre before starting, then to lean on it to use body weight rather than arm strength alone. When throwing large ware the hands are only able to control a small portion of the pot at any one time so an increased level of skill and concentration is required to lift the clay and keep it centralized. For me fashioning a large lump of clay into a huge, glistening fresh pot generous of form, brings a sense of achievement that you just can't get from throwing mugs, jugs and eggcups. If you enjoy decorating, then a large pot will give you a bigger canvas on which to express yourself. Throwing large pots isn't for everyone so it is important to recognize 'your own scale'. For most potters there seems to be a particular size of pot that works best for them and if you work well on intricate porcelain boxes you may not feel quite so much at home with hefty terracotta.

Centring a Large Piece of Clay

With the wheel-head spinning slowly the clay is patted and slapped until it is fairly close to being centred. If the clay is made into a neat ball and well positioned first it should only take a couple of minutes. It's not possible to completely centre the clay by this process, though, so don't be too fussy. With a large piece of clay you can only work on a small section at any one time, so it's often best to mentally divide the clay into two (top and bottom) and approach each section separately. The bottom two or three inches should be completely centred before water is applied and scrapping off the excess clay with the fingertips does this. With the wheel head spinning fairly fast hold the fingertips tight against the bottom of the clay, scrapping off only as much clay as is necessary to centre this section. Water is now applied and the clay is centred from the top down to the bottom; several different hand positions are used although I generally start with the conventional one. The fleshy parts of the palms are used instead of the fingers and forward pressure (sometimes with both hands) is used in preference to sideways pressure. The left leg can be stretched out behind at times to help you really lean on the clay. The most important thing to remember is to use your body weight in preference to arm strength and to get the clay the right shape and fairly well centred before you add any water.

*P*atting the clay to position it in the centre.

*C*entring the bottom.

*C*entring the top.

*U*sing body weight is the best way to centre a large piece of clay.

Opening a Large Piece of Clay

There are two methods used to open a large piece of clay and although the conventional method can be used when making any shape of pot it is best saved for shorter, wider ones. When producing taller pots it is much better to 'bore' the clay. This is a technique where the lump is kept tall and thin when centred, and the top is hollowed slightly in the usual manner so that the fingers can find the centre easily. The fingers are held tightly together and with the wheel spinning fast they are pushed down through the clay through to the wheel-head to produce a thick cylinder. The advantage 'boring' has over the usual technique is that when the clay is opened it will almost be as tall as it would be normally after the first lift. It is a specialized technique generally only used when producing large pots. It can be difficult to keep the hole central when first trying it but it is worth some perseverance, as it will save considerable time and more importantly strain on joints once mastered. If you find it difficult to keep the hole central try inserting your fingers just slightly (about 0.5cm) away from the centre at about '5 o'clock'. Open the clay and form the drainage hole maintaining this distance from the centre. Once the drainage hole is formed the base can be worked on. If the conventional opening method is being used then carry on and make the base in the usual way; if the boring technique is being used then making the base requires slightly more care. With the clay opened to form a thick cylinder it can be difficult to see inside and control exactly what you are doing. Again with perseverance, a feel for how thick and wide to make the base will soon come but until this point is reached, a pair of callipers may come in handy. The aim is to push the base out to its eventual width and form a sharp corner where the base meets the wall of the pot. At the same time it is important to keep the top of the cylinder quite narrow so it can be controlled while lifting.

Lifting a Large Pot

Technically this is the most difficult part to master when throwing a large pot, it requires a degree of strength, a great deal of control and a very steady nerve. It is crucial to get the full height from each lift, as it is very difficult to make up lost height in subsequent lifts. A short thick pot will be more likely to succumb to cracking during the drying and firing process and will also look poorly thrown and underdeveloped. In technical terms the main difference from throwing small pots is that the right thumb is used to 'collar' the pot as the right knuckles are lifting. This has the effect of keeping the pot narrower and therefore under a greater degree of control. Other than this, the method is much the same. It is just that more care and attention must be paid to each step to ensure that it is right before proceeding to the next. It is possible to lift a cylinder to a height in excess of 22in, but on such a tall pot the amount of control you have is limited to a very small proportion at any one time. If the cylinder becomes un-centred it can prove difficult to correct for this reason. Greater control is aided by having the wheel-head spinning quite slowly and by monitoring carefully your every action.

There is an alternative method that was used by many of the old country potters for the first lift on very large pots. Although it is rarely used by many contemporary potters, it is a valid technique and definitely worth a mention. The hands move around to the left-hand side of the pot at about '7 o'clock' with the right hand lifting from the inside and the left hand on the outside. I find it best to use the right fingertips and the heel of the left hand. The technique works on the principle that with the clay spinning in towards the hands (rather than sliding through the hands as the clay does when lifting on the right-hand side) it is easier to apply the considerable pressure that is needed to complete the first lift.

Shaping a Large Pot

This is the final, most crucial and most nerve-wracking stage in throwing a large pot. There is nothing worse than sweating and toiling over a mammoth lump of clay, wedging, centring and lifting it, only to find that your efforts go unrewarded when it ends in a crumpled heap in the wheel tray. As with lifting, the technique is basically the same as that used when throwing a smaller pot (refer to shaping a pot for detailed explanation). One common mistake is made though which seems more prevalent when throwing large wide-bellied or wide-rimmed pots. Often the cylinder is thrown too thinly on the section that is to be widened. This results in the pot either collapsing or the belly or rim not being pushed out to the desired width. To counteract this it is often necessary to throw the cylinder leaving a thicker area where the belly is to

be positioned, or by opening the cylinder to a trumpet shape before the final height is reached in the case of a wide-rimmed pot. It also seems necessary to exaggerate the desired shape slightly; pushing bellies and rims slightly wider than seems visually necessary. I have often unloaded pots from the kiln and been slightly disappointed with the lack of generosity of the forms. They seemed to bear no relation to the fresh, fully formed pots that I had thrown a few weeks previously. The answer is a simple one, the pots had shrunk by about 12 per cent and although they had shrunk evenly the subtle balance between the rim, belly and the foot had been altered. With a large pot maybe shrinking 3–4in, this alteration in the proportions is much more noticeable. When throwing these pots now I try to give them the feeling of being a little plump.

Joining Pots and Throwing Coils

Pots that need to be made from a weight of clay greater than the potter is comfortable with will need to be made in two or more pieces. In any case, weights of more than about 50lb (22kg) or pots taller than 18–20in (46–51cm) are more quickly and efficiently made in sections. Two methods can be used – throwing and joining pots together, which is better for taller narrower pots, particularly if the opening is narrow or throwing coils, which is best suited to wider shapes.

Joining Pots

This was the traditional method of production used by the Renaissance Italian potters when throwing large storage jars, some being over 6ft tall. The bottom part of the pot is thrown first more or less in the usual way. Be sure though not to overstretch the walls – just under the rim is particularly susceptible to this. The rim is then finished off by scoring a fairly deep 'V'-shaped groove into it. (The top part is finished with its rim coming to a point, when the two pieces are assembled they will locate together making a good, strong join).

When the base is finished it should be put aside to dry slightly. Be sure not to place it in a strong draught or in sunlight, which may warp it resulting in the pot being very difficult to assemble. In fact the best way to dry the pot if you have the time (or the luxury of two wheels) is by leaving the base on the wheel revolving slowly with a desk fan directed at it. This ensures quick, even drying and allows you to complete the pot after only a few hours. The pot should be assembled with the top slightly softer, so either dry the base with a fan or throw the top at a later date. For me the best timescale is to throw the bases in an afternoon (maybe up to ten, a greater number involves too much finishing). Then throw the tops the following morning, with both pieces usually being dry enough to assemble later that afternoon.

It's always a fine line judging when the pots are ready to assemble. If they are joined too soon there is a risk that they will collapse, if too late the pot may be too hard to throw in the final shape, or the join may not bond properly and crack when drying. In any case the finishing always takes longer than I anticipate and inevitably I either end up working late into the evening, or wrapping everything to be finished the following day. The top section is made upside down as a bowl without a base and as mentioned earlier with the rim concluding in a point. A measurement can be taken from the rim of the bottom piece with callipers to give a fairly accurate indication of the desired width of the top piece. The two halves seldom seem to fit exactly together though, so one half will have to be widened. I find the best method is to offer the top up to the base to assess which is the wider piece (leave the top section attached to the bat as it's easier to move around). Then place whichever is the narrower section back on the wheel and throw it gently to coax it to the required width. When the two halves fit together accurately slip can be applied to the groove in the bottom section and the top can be placed on. Work the join together to ensure the two pieces are well bonded and apply a very soft thin coil of clay over the seam to disguise it. If the pot is slightly off-centre it can be adjusted by pushing the bat on the top, it's not always possible to completely centre the pot but just do your best. Once fairly satisfied the bat can be cut from the top section. This is slightly awkward and I find that my chin often comes in handy as a support to push against the top bat. With the bat removed, the join on the inside can be worked with a finger, rib or sponge – whatever seems most appropriate, (depending on the firmness of the clay). Then the pot is thrown to give definition to the rim and to ensure the profile of the pot is a continuous sweeping curve. I find it easiest to use a rib and have the wheel spinning very slowly to ensure that complete control is maintained.

Throwing Coils

This is the method used by the ancient Cretan potters when producing their massive grain and oil jars. Today the technique is used by no less a potter than Sven Bayer and is very useful when producing large flared shaped pots, or pots with very wide bellies. The base is made in the usual way with the rim being finished coming to a point, but be sure to throw the form fairly generously as the pot will shrink in before the coil is thrown on it. The base needs to be fairly firm before a coil is added to it so either leave it overnight or dry it with a fan (as described earlier in Joining Pots). When the pot has only a small degree of flexibility is the best condition for joining. Place the base on the wheel and make your best effort to recentre it. If the base has dried unevenly it may need to be 'paddled' with a beater or may be thrown out slightly to do this. Score the rim fairly deeply – I find a fork held against a slowly spinning rim works very well. Smear thick, sticky slip all over the scored area and work it in well to make sure no air is trapped – again I find this easiest to do with the wheel spinning fairly slowly.

The Coil

The dimensions and consistency of the coil are crucial and for this reason it justifies a section devoted especially to it. Throwing the coil is actually fairly simple as long as time is taken to prepare it and centre it on the pot properly. The coil needs to be rolled out from soft clay. If you imagine how soft the wall of a pot is when it is lifted into a cylinder that will give you a good indication. Coils up to 4ft (1.2m) can be rolled out in one piece reasonably comfortably; larger ones will need to be made in two pieces. Before you start to roll the coil make sure your bench is really clean and moisten it slightly so the coil doesn't dry out while it is being rolled. The coil is rolled in the usual manner, firstly by patting and turning it until it is about 3in (7.5cm) in diameter then by rolling it. Be careful not to let the end of the coil become hollow while it is being rolled, as this will give you real problems. When it is smooth and even and approximately 1.5–2in (4–5cm) in diameter it is ready to be placed onto the base.

Make sure the rim is still moist with sticky slip. If not apply a little more, then carefully and gently place the coil onto it. Place the coil so it overhangs mainly on the inside, with maybe a 0.5in overhanging the outside. Cut both ends at 45 degrees and mitre them together to form a good join. The coil now needs to be blended onto the pot, firstly on the outside working it carefully and rhythmically in with the thumb. Then repeat this process on the inside making sure the coil is really well-bonded. The coil now needs to be checked to ensure that it is of a consistent thickness all the way round. Firstly, with the wheel spinning fairly slowly I scrape the coil with the fingertips both inside and out. It is then pinched gently between the thumb and forefinger all of the way round to check that it is of a completely even thickness. When satisfied, (and not before) throwing can begin. The throwing time in relation to the time spent preparing the coil is relatively short. Dribble water onto a fairly slowly spinning rim, grip it between the thumb and fingers of the left hand (fingers inside, thumb outside) and place the right hand on top to add support. Concentrate firstly on centring the coil, when this is accomplished push it in and upwards thinning it slightly as you do so. Any unevenness in the rim can now be trimmed off but if it's minimal ignore it, as it will be lost when the rim is thickened, which is the next step. Thicken and form the final shape of the rim now before any more height is lifted from the wall. The rest of the height and shaping is completed in the conventional way – just bear in mind that the rim will shrink in so it may need to be thrown slightly wider to compensate for this. Once finished, dry the pot slowly with the bottom section wrapped up at least overnight to let the consistency between the two pieces even up. If you are throwing a pot which needs to have more than one coil added to it, finish the rim off coming to a point (as was done with the base). Very large pots indeed can be thrown by this technique. I have thrown pots that weighed in excess of 0.25 of a tonne, 6ft (1.8m) in diameter and made from 12 coils, each one giving me between 4–6in (10–15cm) of height. As long as the pot is wrapped well leaving only the last coil exposed to dry off there is no problem with cracking.

Throwing pots at S & B Evans and Sons.

Repetition Throwing

Although the technique is the same whether throwing one pot or a hundred it is necessary to enter a different frame of mind when repetition throwing. This is definitely aided by a methodical approach and a well-designed and organized workshop. Preparation is the key – clean all necessary work surfaces first before you start to wedge your clay. Prepare enough clay to last you for a morning's throwing. This will then need to be wrapped well so it stays in a good throwing condition. Place the clay within easy reach so you don't have to leave the wheel between making pots. I prefer to have the clay on my left-hand side leaving my right-hand side free for placing pots. Small pots up to 6 or 8lb (2.5kg to 3.5kg) can be placed directly onto ware-boards while larger pots are best placed straight onto racking. The racking should be cleared first so there are no interruptions once throwing has commenced. It is also important to organize your tools and your wheel tray too. Clear most of the slurry, unwanted

tools and dry clay away from the wheel tray and surrounding area before you start throwing. Most pots can be thrown using just a few tools. If you can shape the wall of the pot with the same tool as you trim the bottom it saves time spent on searching for another tool. This may seem petty, but a good production thrower would expect to throw fifty mugs per hour and when throwing in very large batches every second counts. For most pots I use only three tools, a pear-shaped turning tool, a potter's knife and a piece of Perspex ruler cut to about 4in (10cm).

*B*asic tools for repetition throwing.

For small pots I find it easiest to place my tools in the wheel tray at about '9 o'clock' and for larger pots I tend to use a shelf within easy reach to my right. The water pot should be a good size (an ice cream tub works well) and be placed in the back right-hand corner of the wheel tray so that the right hand can access it easily. In summary the basic principles are as follows:

- Design your workshop so it can cope adequately with your volume and scale of production
- Organize your workshop so tasks are performed in a running sequence. That is to say, keep related tasks as close together as possible – for example, clay storage next to wedging, wedging next to throwing, and so on

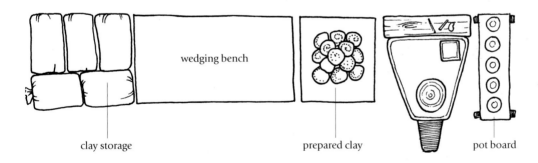

clay storage   wedging bench   prepared clay   pot board

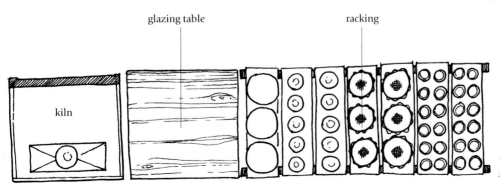

glazing table   racking

kiln

A workshop set up for repetition throwing.

- Clean all surfaces before you start preparation
- Prepare enough clay to last a full session's throwing
- Organize your work space so clay, tools and pot storage are easily accessible without leaving the wheel
- Be clear in your mind what you are going to make before you start.

Throwing on Bats and Tiles

Throwing on Bats

A bat is a round board on which pots are thrown. It is often made of plywood, chipboard or sometimes Asbestolux. They can be attached to the wheel-head by a pad of clay or by pins protruding from it that the bat slots on to. A Lotus wheel-head is specially designed for use with bats; it is recessed allowing them to fit in flush with the level of the wheel-head.

Traditionally country potters would lift pots of any size directly from the wheel-head. Not even stopping the wheel when lifting small pots and using only a cow rib bone to support larger ones. Nowadays terracotta pots have an inherent value attached to them and require potters to strive for a greater degree of 'finish' to satisfy the demands of the modern consumer. Therefore most potters choose to throw pots larger than about 8lb (3.5kg) on bats, the advantage being that pots removed from the wheel on bats will not distort or be covered in messy fingerprints. For large pots bats are best made from board at least 0.5in (1.25cm) thick but 1in (2.5cm) is better. A range of sizes from 12in to 16in (30cm to 40cm) will cater for most pots but a few of about 24in (60cm) always come in useful. Bats larger than about 14in (35cm) may be too wide to fit inside the wheel tray in which case it is necessary to remove the tray. Alternatively, the wheel-head could be built up above the height of the tray by attaching one bat on top of another. A pad of clay is thrown out across the wheel-head and grooves are made with the fingertips. The bat is placed on top and thumped with a fist to ensure that it stays in position.

Throwing on Tiles

Generally most potters seem to prefer to lift small pots directly from the wheel-head and place them onto ware-boards. As I have no desire to turn off excess weight and messy fingerprints from the bases of pots, I find it more convenient to throw fairly thinly onto 6in (15cm) bisque-fired tiles. An additional advantage is that pots do not need to be wired off. They just pop off as they dry due to the porous nature of the tiles, which also aids the quick and even drying of bases. The tiles can be acquired directly from Stoke-on-Trent or from one of the many distributors around the country. A tile bat can be made simply by cutting a tile-sized square hole out of the centre of a 12in (30cm) throwing bat and fixing this to another 12in (30cm) throwing bat. The tile should be held firmly in the recessed area and fit flush with the level of the bat. Throwing on tiles may seem slightly strange at first, and you may find that the tile pops out during the middle of a lift, or you may be put off initially by the uneven surface of the bat. However, it is a good way of producing flowerpots and worth persevering with.

The tile is placed into the recessed tile bat.

The tile is cleaned with a turning tool (below).

Throwing a Pot with a Scalloped Rim

As with many traditional flowerpot designs, the scalloped rimmed pot is decorated while still on the wheel-head, immediately after being thrown. For this reason it is quick to produce and as it doesn't need to be fiddled with after leaving the wheel it is left looking crisp and fresh once completed.

*T*he clay is patted to position it in the centre.

*C*entring the clay (below).

*O*pening the clay.

*F*orming the base of
the pot.

*T*he pot is pushed in
to form a cone shape.

*T*he top is collared to
keep it even.

The wall of the pot is lifted.

The foot of the pot is shaped with a pear-shaped turning tool.

A '*V*'-shaped groove is formed into the rim with the edge of a ruler.

*F*orming the belly of the pot.

*T*he scallops are now made, the rim is supported with the thumb and index finger of the left hand. The right index finger works the rim down to form the scallop. The process is the same as forming the lip of a jug.

A band of coloured slip is painted onto the belly of the pot (below).

A pattern is applied to the slip with a comb (below right).

If the pot is thrown on a tile, a knife is run around the edge of the rim to ensure that the pot releases easily as it dries (above).

The finished pot.

Throwing a Sprigged Pot

The decoration on this pot is very quick and simple to do – it only requires a few simple press moulds. It is a very effective way of giving your work a more elaborate and personalized feel.

The clay is patted to position it close to the centre.

The base of the pot is centred.

Centring the side of the pot (above).

Centring the top of the pot.

Opening out the centre lump.

Forming the base.

The base of the pot is compressed.

The cylinder is now collared.

The wall of the pot is rouletted with a pastry cutter (above).

The finished pot is left to stiffen.

A plaster mould is
held against the pot
and the wall of the pot
is pushed into it.

*T*he finished pot.

Throwing a Large Strawberry Pot

This magnificent pot is in the repertoire of most gardenware makers. Large strawberry pots will need to be made in two sections and joined when they have dried out slightly. Making the base:

*T*he clay is patted (above left).

*U*se body weight to centre the clay (above).

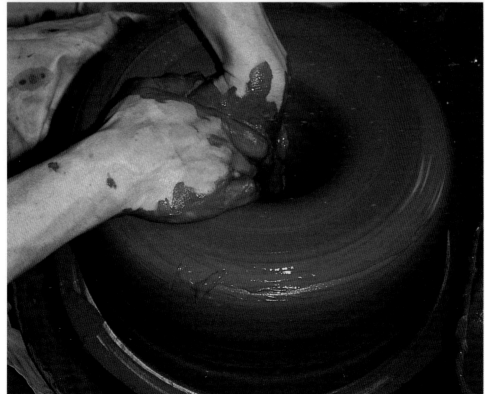

*O*pening out the pot.

*F*orming the base (right).

*S*tarting to lift the pot (far right).

*T*he first lift.

*T*he second lift
(above left).

*T*he third lift
(above).

*T*he pot is shaped
on the fourth lift.

A '*V*'-*shaped groove is scored into the rim.*

M*AKING THE TOP SECTION*

*T*his is thrown upside down like a bowl, and made without a base.*

*T*he width of the rim is checked (above left).

*W*hen it is nearly at its final measurement the base (that will become the rim of the pot) is trimmed (above).

*I*t is now eased out to its final width and the rim is made to come to a point.

*W*hen the base has dried it is returned to the wheel, and slip is applied to the rim (above).

*T*he top section is now placed onto the base (still attached to the bat it is easier to handle) (above right).

*T*he join is now worked together and a thin coil is added to hide the seam.

*T*he bat is removed and the rim is shaped (above left).

*T*he belly of the pot is now thrown to make the shape of the pot full and continuous (above).

A 'pastry' coil is added under the rim.

*T*he pastry effect is accomplished by pushing the coil rhythmically with the index finger while the pot spins slowly.

*T*he Strawberry pockets are marked out.

*T*he pockets are cut with a knife, alternatively a finger can be worked from side to side to form a hole.

*W*ork the lip of the pocket out with a wet finger.

The finished pot.

Throwing a Large Swagged Pot

The technique of throwing coils allows enormous scope in terms of form and enables you to produce pots of magnificent proportions that make a real statement in the garden environment.

Opening out the clay.

*F*orming the base (above).

*T*he palm of the hand is used to lift (above right).

*T*he second lift.

On the third lift the pot is opened slightly at the top.

A rib is used to continue the widening of the rim.

The pot is left to dry until it is soft leather hard. It is then returned to the wheel and the rim is scored with a fork (below).

Thick slurry is now applied (below right).

*T*he coil is carefully laid onto the rim of the pot.

*T*he join is mitred to make sure the join is strong and even (far left).

*T*he outside of the coil is smoothed onto the pot with a downwards motion of the fingers (left).

The inside of the coil is now smoothed in the same way.

With the wheel spinning slowly the coil is scraped with the fingertips to ensure it is centralized and even.

*W*ater is now applied and throwing can commence.

*T*he coil is now lifted inwards and upwards.

*A*ny unevenness in the rim can now be trimmed (right).

*T*he rim of the pot is formed by pushing it down with the index finger (far right).

*T*he rim is given its final shape (below).

*T*he coil is given a final lift (below right).

*T*he coil is shaped and smoothed with a rib (far left).

*A*ny necessary final adjustments are made to the rim (left).

*T*he finished pot. For a detailed description of how to apply swags see 'Making a Large Moulded Urn'.

4 Press-Moulded Pots

It is a fact often forgotten that long before the Industrial Revolution potters were using moulding as a method of production. Many British country potteries used it more than a century ago to produce 'vases', (their term for a decorative flowerpot). It was perhaps best exploited though by the Italian Renaissance potters who produced huge urns highly decorated with draped swags and garlands. These traditional methods used extensively by artists such as Luca Della Robbia in the mid-fifteenth century are still very much alive today in Tuscan villages such as Impruneta.

Press moulding allows you to produce pots, urns, troughs and figurative pieces of any shape and size. Once 'Master forms' have been made, often painstakingly, with extremely intricate detail, working moulds can be taken. With these moulds even semi-skilled workers can produce highly decorative pots quickly. Throwing by comparison restricts you to the cylinder, decoration has to be applied to each pot individually and pieces larger than about 24in by 24in (60cm by 60cm) become quite a serious project. During this chapter we will be looking at how to produce 'master forms', working moulds and finally, finished pots from these moulds.

Making a Master Form

This is the original pot or form that working moulds are made from. It can be made of any solid material – wood, plastic, metal, plaster and polystyrene for instance are all suitable. As I am most comfortable working in clay though, I generally try to use it wherever possible, although on occasions it can be useful to combine materials. When making troughs for example, it may be easier to construct the basic form from wood and model the rim and other details on in clay. It can also be worthwhile scouring garden centres for cheap plastic pots that are similar to your requirements. Clay can be modelled, or even thrown onto them relatively quickly to change them into pots that are individual and personal to you. If you are making your master forms from clay, then the usual clay working practices that we have to adhere to do not restrain you. It is not necessary to throw pots thinly, or join clay pieces together only when it is the same consistency. The master will not be fired, it will be discarded once a mould is made. It is actually beneficial to make 'masters' thicker than normal so they are stronger – if necessary they can even be made solid. The most important points to remember are: take plenty of time to consider the exact range of moulded pots you want, and only start to make the masters when you have exact shape and sizes clear in your mind. Be painstakingly specific over the smallest details as it takes considerable effort to produce the master forms and working moulds. You will not want to go to the trouble of remaking them if they are not quite right. Be sure to make the masters strong enough to withstand the weight of plaster that will be poured over them. This is particularly important if the master form is made from clay and will be cast in a leather hard state. Whenever possible, try to avoid undercuts on your master forms, as this will result in more complex moulds having to be made. Sometimes they are unavoidable but it is always preferable to keep the moulds as simple as possible. On occasions it may be necessary to sprig the decoration on separately.

Making Working Moulds

Wood, metal, bisque-fired clay and plaster of Paris are all suitable materials from which to make working moulds but plaster is generally the most appropriate and widely used of them. It is relatively inexpensive and for complex shapes the easiest material to use. The major advantage plaster has is its high degree of absorbency. The surface of the clay is dried quickly causing the pot to shrink and release from the mould. Having said this, for those of you who encounter plaster only fairly rarely the experience can be a fretful, even harrowing one. There is nothing more annoying and frustrating than when your carefully constructed mould starts to ooze smooth wet plaster from a not so carefully constructed seam. I certainly have had this experience and the only answer seems to be to take a 'belt and braces approach'. Retaining walls made of clay are only considered for very small moulds, with wooden frames nailed or screwed together and sealed with a clay coil inside and out being the usual practice.

When making working plaster moulds for slip cast wares the usual practice is to make master moulds from a very hard plaster and take the working moulds from these. The working moulds have a fairly short life expectancy and new ones can be produced quite simply from the masters. I choose not to adopt this approach – it works very well when producing small pots in vast quantities. My press-moulded pots in contrast tend to be quite large and master moulds would take up an enormous amount of space. As I only produce these pots in reasonably small quantities each mould would last several years by which time I would generally need to update my range anyway.

As I am a potter by training and not a mould-maker my approach when making moulds is to keep the process as simple as possible. I always make moulds in as few pieces as I can get away with; this can often mean even casting the pot in one piece then carefully sawing the mould in half when it has 'gone off' to create a simple two piece mould. The width of the saw cut is lost from the mould but on large pots this loss is negligible. Instead of natches (locating lugs), lines are scored onto the mould, which bisect the saw cut, and these can be matched up to align the mould correctly. The assembled mould is bound tightly normally top and bottom with heavy cord to keep it in place. This way of making moulds would not be suitable if you intended to cast fine bone china, but it can be a good method for making moulds for large, heavily grogged flowerpots. Ultimately it is for you to decide whether or not and how much you want to compromise. It is a decision that should be based on:

- Your own level of competency – if you are not that experienced start by making your moulds as simple as possible
- How much time you can spare – if you're running your own business then time spent on research and development can eat into time that you would rather spend on production
- The detail and size of the mould – if the mould is very detailed and fairly small then more care may have to be taken to make your moulds accurately.

Mixing Plaster

As long as a few basic principles are observed mixing plaster is fairly straightforward. The recommended ratio of plaster to water is 5lb (2.2kg) plaster to 3 pints (1.7l) water.

Most professional mould-makers never actually use any measurements though preferring instead to rely on a rule of thumb. The method for mixing plaster without measurements is as follows:

1. Half fill a bowl or bucket with cold water.
2. Gently sprinkle the plaster onto the surface of the water trying to avoid dropping large lumps into the container. When the plaster has become saturated with water and sunk add more plaster. It is very important not to be tempted to mix it with your hand at this stage. Keep adding plaster until an island forms just above the surface of the water.

3. Gently kick the bottom of the container to encourage the plaster to sink. As the plaster absorbs water, air bubbles will rise to the surface. Keep kicking the container until these are all expelled.
4. Gently agitate the plaster from the bottom with your hand until it feels smooth, creamy and well mixed together.
5. Pour immediately as the plaster will soon thicken and start to set.

Surplus plaster should never be poured down a sink or drain. It is best poured onto sheets of newspaper and disposed of when it has set.

Plaster, which is very old or damp should not be used, moulds made from it generally tend to be very soft and deteriorate quickly. If you intend to keep plaster for more than a few days make sure it is stored in a warm dry place.

Making a Simple Two-piece Trough Mould

*C*lay is smeared thinly on the surface of the plastic trough to hide its fluted decoration (below).

Here a simple trough mould is made by adapting a cheap plastic trough bought in a local garden centre.

*T*he surface is smoothed with a sponge (above right).

A coil is added to the inside of the rim and a wooden frame is placed around the trough.

Making the Master and the Working Mould

Once dry, notches are made by carving a recess with a teaspoon. The surface of the plaster is coated with soft soap so the second piece of mould will release easily.

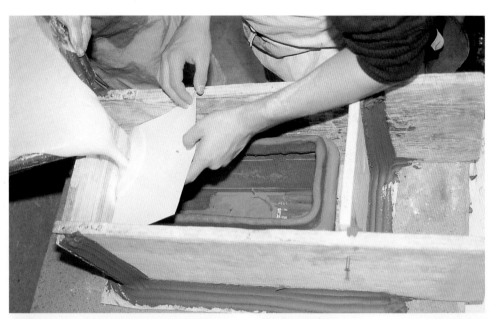

*P*laster is poured up to the lower edge of the rim.

*O*nce dry, notches are made by carving a recess with a teaspoon. The surface of the plaster is coated with soft soap so the second piece of mould will release easily (below left).

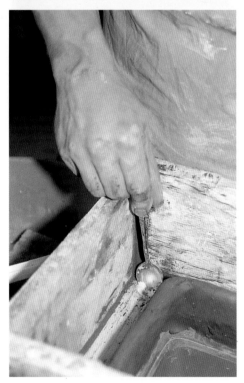

*T*he second section is poured to a height of at least 1in above the rim. After a couple of hours the mould can be separated and cleaned up. Dry the mould thoroughly before use (right).

MAKING AND
DECORATING
THE TROUGH

*Slabs of clay are
patted into the
mould from the
bottom upwards.*

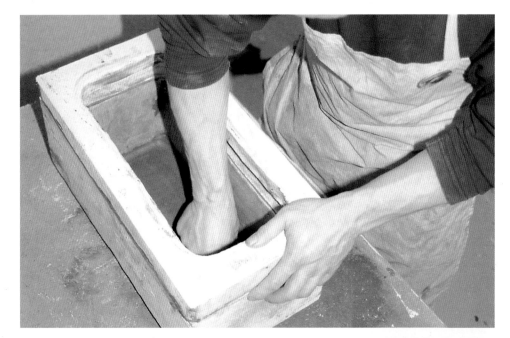

*Leave the trough in
the mould overnight
then flip the mould
over and let it drop
out.*

*T*idy the trough by
scraping with a rib and
smoothing with
a sponge.

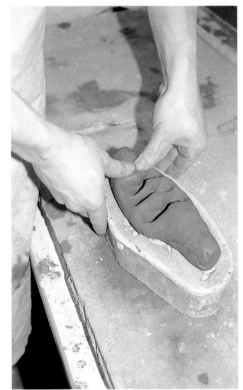

*T*o make the
decoration, a sausage
of clay is placed onto
the mould (far left).

*T*he clay is pressed
with the fingertips
(left).

*B*ash the clay with a fist (right).

*R*emove the clay carefully (far right).

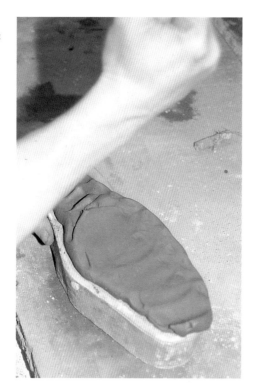

*C*ut the decoration off with a thin wire.

*S*core the side of the trough and fix the decoration on with slip. Clean away any surplus slip and wipe lightly with a wet sponge.

*T*he finished trough.

Making a Large Moulded Urn

This large moulded urn is made in a two-piece mould. The mould was originally made in one piece then cut in half with a handsaw to form a simple two-piece mould.

*S*labs need to be made to fill the mould. They can be made to a standard size and thickness very simply in a wooden mould. Place a piece of strong plastic into the bottom of the mould and bash a slab of clay into the mould with a brick. Cut the surplus clay off with a wire and cut around the edge of the slab with a knife. The slab should now drop out easily.

T*he slabs are placed into the mould. They are overlapped slightly and the seams are bashed together with a fist to make a good join (above).*

A *coil is placed into the mould to form the rim.*

The last few slabs are patted into the mould to complete the form.

The inside of the mould is smoothed with a rib.

*T*he pot is left in the mould for two days to stiffen.

*T*he pot is put on the wheel and the seams and blemishes are filled with soft clay. With the wheel revolving slowly the pot is smoothed with a wooden rib (below).

*S*wags are placed onto the pot. When the positioning is correct the swags are scored round and removed.

*T*he pot is scored quite deeply with a fork.

*T*he swags are pushed firmly onto the pot, any spare slip is then wiped off with a wet sponge (above).

*T*he pot is left to dry slightly before the detail is modelled back on.

*R*ough edges are
taken off with a wet
brush.

*T*he finished pot.

5 Decoration

It is often said that simplicity is the essence of all good design and this is certainly true in the case of the traditional tapered flowerpot. Not only is it the most economic shape to produce, in terms of kiln packing and delivering, being tapered it makes an ideal plant container. Plants can be removed easily to 'pot them on' and it is wide enough at the base to make it stable. However the modern potter must concern himself with more than just purely function. A well-designed pot will achieve a balance between aesthetic considerations and the purpose for which it is intended. Although one or two unusual containers can be found planted up in most gardens (Victorian chimney pots, china teapots, wheelbarrows) the most appropriate shape is based on the standard tapered flowerpot.

In order to produce a range of work that sets you apart from the crowd and allows you a degree of self-expression, it is necessary to design pots that are creative, original and personal. As the range of forms suitable for flowerpots is fairly limited this is best achieved through decoration. Many different forms and styles of decoration can be applied to gardenware. The main consideration is that the decoration should complement the planting and not overpower it. Bright, bold and busy planting for example often suits a fairly plain or simple pot, while very ornate pots limit the possible planting options. Types of decoration that are applied to a freshly thrown pot fairly quickly and simply are therefore well suited to plant pots. These include piecrust, scalloped, combed and rouletted decorations. Examples of all of these types of decoration can be found in the throwing section.

Comb rhythmically with the wheel spinning slowly (below).

Lines are scored to frame the decoration (below right).

Combing

Combing provides a very quick, simple and free-flowing form of decoration. It works especially well if the combing is performed immediately onto a band of wet coloured

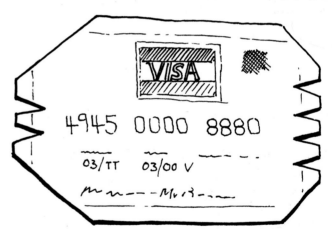

slip. Combs can be made quite simply by cutting teeth into a credit card, piece of hard wood or metal.

Roulettes

Most of my pots have a simple rouletted pattern applied to them with a pastry cutter. It has become a faithful companion

*T*rim the bottom with a knife (above left).

*T*he finished decoration (above right).

A credit card comb (above).

*D*etail of rouletted pattern (left).

*R*ouletted patterns.

*U*sing a roulette
(below).

A simple stamp
(below right).

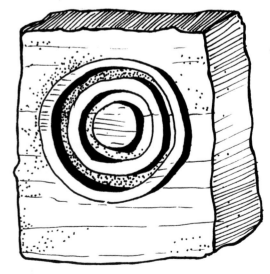

over the many years I have used it and I'm sure I would be lost without it. With a little care and patience roulettes can be made to your own design. Choose a repeating pattern – it does not need to be very complicated; often simple patterns made of circles or triangles for instance, can be very effective. A small plaster stamp of the pattern is made, this is either carved into a block of plaster or a plaster cast is taken from a clay model. The roulette wheel is then made, this can be thrown quite simply. It is made like a plant pot saucer and has a hollow stem attached to its centre. When leather-hard the pattern is stamped around its outside wall with the small plaster mould made earlier. Once biscuit-fired, the roulette wheel is mounted onto a turning tool and is then ready for use. Be sure to soak it in water before each usage or it will stick to the surface of the pot. The decoration may appear quite messy at first but this will soon be overcome with a little practice. It is often simply a question of applying the decoration with the correct amount of pressure or holding the roulette at the correct angle.

*T*wo roulettes.

Sprigs

To apply relief decoration that is particularly bold or detailed it is necessary to use sprig moulds. Plaster moulds can be made for each different type of decoration you use.

Large or heavy sprigs will need to be pressed out of the mould separately and stuck onto a pot (when it is soft leather hard) with slip. To make sure the bond between pot and sprig is strong it is best to let the sprig dry until it is as stiff as the pot. The pot is then scored quite deeply, smeared with slip and the sprig is then pushed on fairly hard to squeeze out any surplus slip. This is wiped off and any detail lost will need to be modelled back on. For a more detailed description *see* Throwing a Large Swagged Pot (page 71). If the decoration is not quite so heavy, it is possible to place the mould to the side of the pot and press the wall of the pot into the mould. The mould needs to be saturated before use to prevent it from sticking to the pot and a feel for knowing where to press to get a clean, crisp image soon comes with a little experience. This method has the advantage of being much quicker to apply and there is also no chance of the sprig falling off, which can be a problem if 'stuck on' sprigs are not applied properly.

*T*he mould.

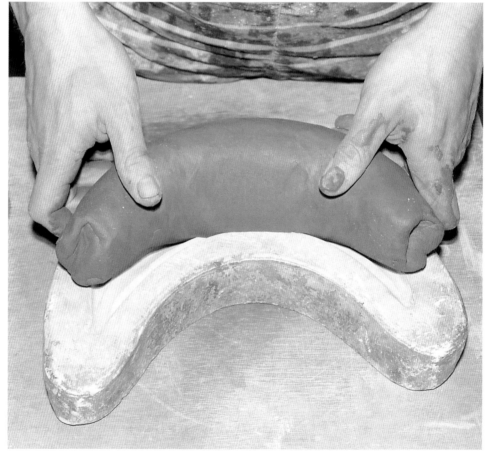

A plug of clay is placed onto the mould.

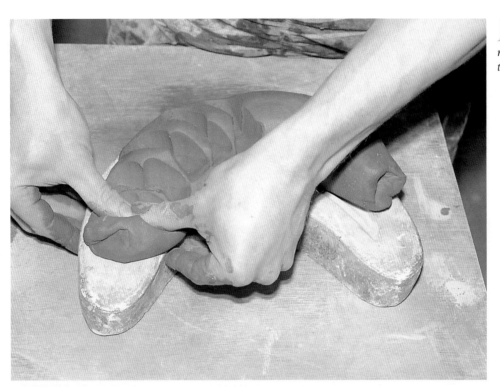

*P*ush the clay into the mould fairly hard with the thumbs.

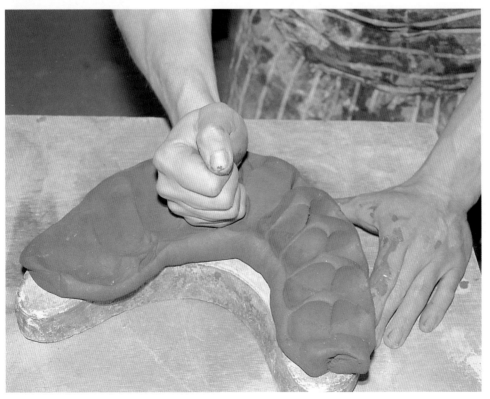

*B*ash the clay into the mould with a fist.

*C*arefully peel the
swag from the mould.

*C*ut the sprig off
with a thin wire.

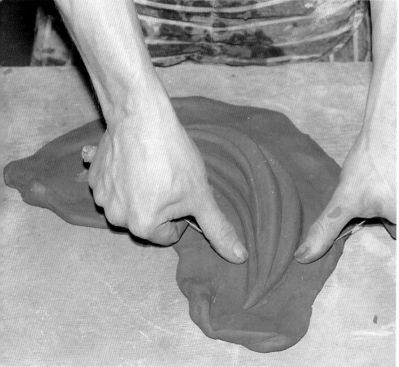

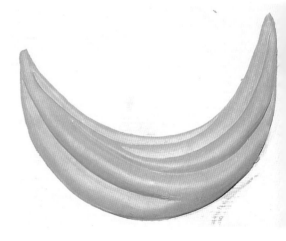

*T*he finished sprig (above).

*S*mall moulds are
often best stamped
onto a coil and cut off
carefully with a thin
wire.

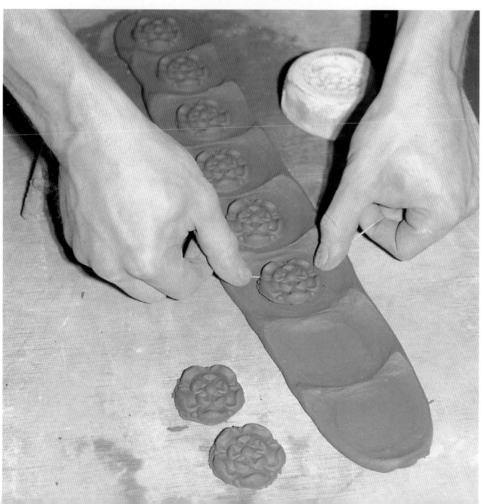

Making a Simple Sprig Mould

*T*he result of using an
olive-leaf sprig mould.

Here an olive leaf sprig mould is being made. Simple sprig moulds like this can be made in just a few hours and used to decorate thousands of pots. Use a harder plaster than the standard potter's plaster to ensure that the mould does not deteriorate too quickly. The decoration is modelled from fairly soft clay but the detail is carved into it when it is much drier,

*T*he original decoration is modelled.

A small retaining wall is placed around the mould.

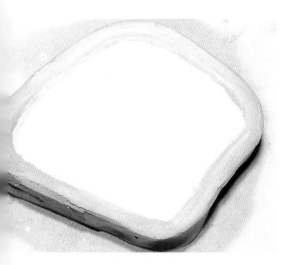

just before it changes colour. I use a knife and a selection of modelling tools to apply the detail and a dry brush to take off any burrs that form. Occasionally the model is wetted lightly with a brush or a sponge to prevent it from drying too much.

Slip and Glaze Trailing

Slip and glaze decoration can enrich and enliven an otherwise plain pot. It will give your range of work more variety and make your displays more interesting. Glazed pots are also more versatile as they are suitable for indoor and outdoor planting. Trailing

Plaster is poured onto the mould. It is then vibrated to expel any air bubbles (above left).

The finished mould should be left to dry at least overnight before it is used (above).

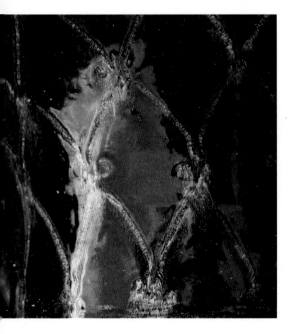

can be quite a time-consuming way of decorating unless it is kept fairly simple. I try to decorate pots on the wheel-head as much as possible by using a series of banded straight and wavy lines. A few dots and squiggles are added to these basic patterns to give them more interest. The use of coloured slips that complement one another or glazes that react with one another (such as bleeding) will liven up even simple decoration. I apply slips to pots at the leather-hard stage and decorate them when they have dried enough not to be damaged by fingerprints. Wherever possible I apply glazes to raw pots and raw fire them. Some raw glazes need to be applied to leather-hard pots while others are best applied to dry pots. Most recipes (including all the recipes in this book) will note the correct time for application.

Ageing Terracotta

Plain terracotta can be enlivened by staining it to make it look weathered. The process is quite straightforward to perform which makes it a good way to set your pots apart from the mass-produced imports. The stain I use is made from terracotta slurry and manganese dioxide. Although it isn't permanent it will last for a few months by which time the natural ageing process will take over.

The stain is applied with a sponge.

Once dry the stain is wiped off with a damp sponge.

6 Drying and Firing

Drying

Put simply the slower a pot is dried the less risk there is of it warping and cracking. As clay dries it shrinks by roughly 12 per cent; if the drying is too rapid and therefore uneven, tremendous stress is placed upon a pot sometimes causing it to crack. In practice though due to limited workshop space and pressure of orders, it is often necessary to push wares through the kiln as often as possible. Unfortunately there are no hard and fast answers as to how quickly pots can be dried. A routine that minimizes losses can only be developed through experience over a period of time. This routine will vary according to the size of the workshop, the characteristics of the clay body and the size and shape of pots being produced. As a rough guide though in my own workshop my preferred drying cycle is as follows (it may be quicker on those occasions when finished pots are urgently required):

Small pots (up to 4lb) (2kg) 1–3 days
Medium pots (15–30lb) (7–14kg) 7–14 days
Large pots (40–55lb) (18–25kg) 14–21 days
Large joined and moulded pots at least 1 month

The choice of clay body is vitally important – for small pots I use a standard smooth terracotta body based on an Etruria marl. For all pots above 6lb (2.7kg) I add 20 per cent sand to this body. For large press-moulded pots I use the sanded body plus 15 per cent large grog (8–Dust). For more information *see* the section on grog (page 19).

Firing

Traditionally country potteries produced a huge volume of pots on an annual basis. Lines of throwers would each make up to a tonne of pots per day. In order to keep up with this scale of production the kilns were massive. Normally fired by wood or coal, they would take up to a week to fire and use many tonnes of fuel. Due to technical advances and more modest scales of production, the modern potter has adopted new kiln designs, materials, fuels and firing cycles. Gas and electric are now the most common fuels and the use of lightweight kiln-building materials with high insulation properties is widespread. If you are looking to buy a kiln for production gardenware then one that can hold a week or maybe two weeks' worth of production is about the right size, with a smaller one about 10–15 cu ft to use for special orders. The choice of fuel (gas or electric) is a personal decision but as a general rule, for new kilns up to 16 cu ft, top-loading electric kilns provide good value, they can be bought cheaply from suppliers such as Cromartie Kilns Ltd. While kilns of 30 cu ft and over are often cheaper to buy second-hand if fired by gas. Kilns can also be built fairly simply to your own requirement but for the purpose of this book I will confine this chapter just to firing cycles. Excellent kiln building information can be found in a number of publications, for instance F. Olsen's *Kiln Book, Pioneer Pottery* and *The Self Reliant Potter*.

Although firing gardenware is broadly speaking similar to other types of ceramics it requires several particular considerations:

Kiln Pack

As in bisque firings, unglazed pots can be packed much more densely. Either rim to rim, packed inside each other or in bungs. This will obviously allow more pots to be fired in a given space.

Firing Cycle

Although this practice of packing densely is more economical, it does require considerable care. The denser the amount of clay packed in the kiln the more water there is to be driven off, which increases the risk of cracking and deforming. To allow for this the firing cycle must be slowed, particularly in the early stages (up to 250°C). As an extra precaution very thick or very large pieces would benefit from a period in a drying room or above the kiln. If pots are telescoped together in a bung or packed inside each other bear in mind that water vapour must be given time to migrate through several layers of clay.

Kiln Ventilation

With a large amount of water vapour being given off up to 450°C it is important to ensure that the kiln is sufficiently well ventilated. Dampers and kiln bungs may need to be opened throughout this period.

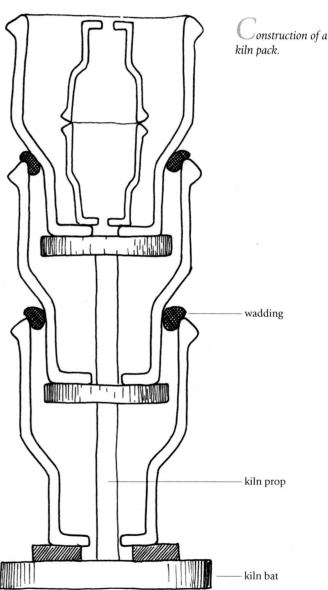

Construction of a kiln pack.

wadding

kiln prop

kiln bat

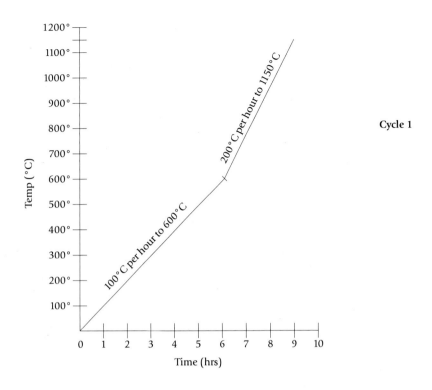

Cycle 1

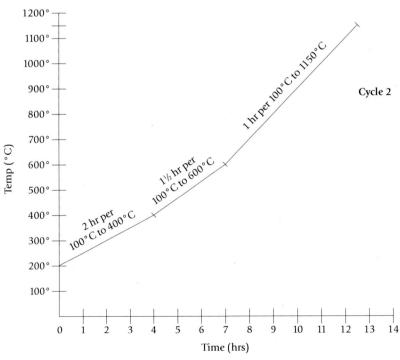

Cycle 2

*T*wo kiln cycles.

pre-heat the kiln overnight to 200°C

Most terracotta gardenware is fired between 1000–1150°C; the exact temperature is determined by the point at which a particular clay vitrifies. Clays based on an Etruria Marl will mature at close to 1150°C and have a wide firing range while clays such as Fremington's Terracotta will mature at around 1000°C and have a very narrow firing range. In fact, over firing Fremingtons by even as little as 10–20°C may cause it to bloat and slump. The fired qualities and attributes of your clay body is an important consideration in your choice of clay. Chapter 2 describes the nature and preparation of clay for gardenware. Trial and error will establish good working practices. By experimenting with additions to your clay body and the drying and firing cycle it should be possible to produce most pots with a high degree of success. Listed on the previous page are two different firing cycles I use. Cycle 1 is used when the kiln is packed with small ware (up to 15lb/7kg) that is thoroughly dry when packed. Cycle 2 is used for larger pots if they are slightly damp or particularly thick and heavy. Both cycles are equally well suited to gas or electric firings.

S & B Evans 16 cu ft top-loading kiln. They use two kilns of this size and a gas-fired kiln of 50 cu ft.

The cooling cycle is important too; large pots, particularly if cooled quickly have a tendency to 'dunt'. This is a crack that occurs during cooling. It often takes the form of a thin, hairline crack travelling almost the whole of the vertical length of the pot. Dunting can often go unnoticed as the cracks are so fine, the best method of detection is to give the pot a knock with a knuckle – if the ring is dull and dead then it may well be cracked. This problem is easily prevented – cooling the kiln slowly is all that is required. For large kilns or densely packed kilns it may just be a question of 'clamming' the kiln up properly (closing the damper, bungs and blocking off burner ports). For small lightweight kilns it may be necessary to fire the kiln down. The temperature range within which dunting is likely to occur is between 600–150°C below which point the kiln is safe to open.

Frost-Proofing Terracotta

When selling gardenware you need to be safe in the knowledge that your pots will not succumb to frost in the first few winters. A bad reputation spreads very quickly, so it's important to produce a reliable range of work in order to run

*The author
unloading the kiln
after a glaze firing.*

your business successfully. Making my pots frost-proof allows me to give a 10-year guarantee, this is a good sales pitch and I'm sure it has clinched many sales.

In practice making pots frost-proof is actually quite simple. It is achieved by firing pots to the point just before 'vitrification'. This will make them strong enough to withstand the severity of winter conditions but they will still retain some porosity, so plant roots will not become waterlogged and rotten. A porous pot will also allow water to evaporate through its walls so roots will be kept cooler during the summer months. For most commercial clays the correct firing temperature is 1100–1150°C, local clay may be anywhere between 1000°C and 1150°C. For a quick indication a low-fired pot can be scratched with a nail and will be very porous, (place the tip of your tongue on the pot to see if it sticks). A high-fired pot generally has a good strong colour and when placed on the palm of your hand and knocked with a knuckle it will have a good high-pitched ring like a bell. Vitrification can be accurately tested for by boiling a fired test tile in water. It is weighed before and afterwards to test for water absorption – if the weight is the same then the tile is vitrified.

The temperature at which a pot needs to be fired to be frost-proof can be reduced by the addition of Flyash or Pulverized Fuel Ash (PFA). This is a waste material produced by coal-burning power stations. Fine grade Flyash can be added in quantities of up to 25 per cent, which results in pots maturing around 100°C lower.

Fountains and other items which will be soaked in water all winter will need some extra help to withstand freezing conditions. Before installation they can be painted with a weather seal (as used on exterior brickwork). This is completely invisible but will make the objects totally waterproof.

7 Clay Bodies and Glaze Recipes

The following recipes have been selected from those that I have used or have been used by friends of mine in the trade. Although they are reliable recipes be sure to test them before mixing up large quantities. Materials may vary from one supplier to another. The type of kiln, fuel and firing cycle can also produce different results. Some fine-tuning may be necessary to make them suitable for your requirements.

The ingredients are calculated by weight unless otherwise indicated and temperature is calibrated in Orton cones. Glazes should be applied to bisque ware which has been fired to Orton cone 07 (973°C).

Clay Bodies

As a general rule I tend to prefer a smooth ungrogged terracotta body for throwing small pots up to 3lb (1.4kg), for pots up to 40lb (18kg) I use an Etruria marl with 10–20 per cent sand added to it. For very large thrown pots I use the sanded body and increase the sand content to at least 25 per cent. For large moulded pots I use the standard sanded body with the addition of about 15 per cent 8–Dust grog. Terracotta glazed pots up to 10lb (4.5kg) are thrown from the smooth body, larger glazed pots are made from the sanded body. Stoneware glazed pots are made from a mix of a smooth iron-bearing stoneware and a highly grogged 'crank' body.

Grog

I use grog supplied by Alpha Whitfield who grade their grogs in millimetres. For large moulded pots I use 5mm–10mm. They also supply grogs in the following grades: 10mm–5mm, 5mm–2mm, 2mm–0mm, 2mm–0.6mm and 600μm.

Slips

The following recipes should be sieved twice through a 120-mesh sieve and applied to leather-hard clay.

BASIC WHITE SLIP

| Ball Clay (HVAR) | 50 |
| China Clay | 50 |

10 per cent–20 per cent of the throwing body can be added to ensure a good fit. This will, however, make the slip a creamy colour if red clay is used.

WHITE SLIP

Ball Clay
China Clay (all three in equal parts)
Flint

Harder and whiter than the above slip, the throwing body can be added if necessary for the same reason.

WHITE VITREOUS SLIP

Ball Clay	35
China Clay	25
Borax Frit E	20
Flint	20

If the Ball Clay and China Clay is calcined by firing it to 1100°C it can be applied to bisque fired pots.

The above white slip recipes can be coloured by adding metal oxides in the following quantities.

Cobalt Carbonate	2.5 per cent produces mid-blue
Cobalt Carbonate	5 per cent produces strong blue
Copper Carbonate	3 per cent produces soft green
Copper Carbonate	7 per cent produces strong green

Other Coloured Slip Recipes

GREEN SLIP

Red Clay	40
Ball Clay	40
Flint	20
Copper Carbonate	2.25
Chrome Oxide	1

BLUE SLIP

Red Clay	80
Flint	20
Cobalt Oxide	1.5
Nickel Oxide	1

IRON SLIP

| Red Clay | 100 |
| Red Iron Oxide | 8 |

IRON SLIP

Ball Clay	51
Flint	40
Crocus Martis	9

BLACK SLIP

Red Clay	80
White Slip	20
Manganese Dioxide	4
Red Iron Oxide	12

BLACK SLIP

Red Clay	100
Manganese Carbonate	6
Cobalt Carbonate	1.5
Nickel Oxide	1

Earthenware Glaze Recipes

CLEAR GLAZE 1020–1040°C

Lead Bisilicate	41
Standard Borax Frit	50
China Clay	9

Apply fairly thinly.

CLEAR GLAZE 1050–1060°C

Lead Bisilicate	70
Low Expansion Frit (P2246)	15
China Clay	15

Apply fairly thinly.

KENNETH CLARK'S CLEAR GLAZE 1060–1080°C

Lead Sesquisilicate	52.8
Potash Feldspar	31.1
Whiting	5.6
China Clay	7.2
Flint	3.3

HONEY GLAZE 1040°C

Lead Sesquisilicate	85
China Clay	10
Flint	5
Red Iron Oxide	4

Apply fairly thickly to bisque ware. A rich deep honey with a highly glossy surface.

HONEY GLAZE 1080–1100°C

Lead Sesquisilicate	8.6
Potash Feldspar	0.5
Flint	0.5
Whiting	0.25
China Clay	1.4
Red Iron Oxide	0.15
Iron Spangles	0.175

A good glaze, highly glossy.
The spangles produce beautiful streaks.

LEAD/ZINC MATT 1060°C

Lead Bisilicate	67
Potash Feldspar	9
Zinc Oxide	19
Quartz	4
Bentonite	1

MATT 1080–1100°C

Lead Bisilicate	40
Alkaline Frit	15
Whiting	5
Zinc Oxide	5
Potash Feldspar	20
China Clay	15

MATT WHITE 1120–1140°C

Lead Bisilicate	70
Low Expansion Frit	15
China Clay	15
Barium Carbonate	15
Whiting	5

WHITE SATIN MATT 1120–1140°C

Lead Sesquisilicate	70
Low Expansion Frit	15
China Clay	15
Tin Oxide	4
Zinc Oxide	4
Titanium Dioxide	4

TIN GLAZE 1060–1080°C

Lead Bisilicate	36
E Frit	24
China Clay	10
Tin Oxide	5
Zinc Oxide	20

TIN GLAZE 1060–1140°C

Lead Bisilicate	60
Standard Borax Frit	9
Cornish Stone	15
China Clay	5
Tin Oxide	8
Zirconium Silicate	6
Zinc Oxide	2
Bentonite	2

MORGAN HALL'S TIN GLAZE 1140°C

Lead Bisilicate	56
Flint	8
Cornish Stone	10
Standard Borax Frit	8
Zinc Oxide	4
Tin Oxide	8
Lithium Carbonate	5

Raw Glaze Recipes

Many glazes can be converted into raw glazes by substituting the China Clay content for Ball Clay. If the China Clay content is less than 15 per cent then the addition of 3 per cent Bentonite to the Ball Clay may be necessary.

RAW CLEAR GLAZE 1080°C

Lead Bisilicate	80
Red Clay	20
Flint	5
Bentonite	3

Apply thickly to leather-hard clay, due to the red clay content it will make white slips a slightly warmer colour.

RAW CLEAR GLAZE 1100°C

Lead Bisilicate	42.5
Standard Borax Frit	32.5
Red Clay	15
Potash Feldspar	10
Bentonite	4

Apply medium thickness to leather-hard or dry clay – due to the red clay content it will make white slips appear a slightly warmer colour.

RAW CLEAR GLAZE 1100–1120°C

Lead Bisilicate	42
Standard Borax Frit	9
Ball Clay (HVAR)	9
Whiting	3

Apply fairly thinly to dry clay.

RAW CLEAR GLAZE 1080–1115°C

Lead Bisilicate	74
Ball Clay	13
Flint	9
Whiting	4

Best soaked for 1 hour, best applied to dry clay.

RAW HONEY GLAZE 1060–1080°C

Lead Bisilicate	80
Red Clay	20
Flint	5
Red Iron Oxide	3
Bentonite	3

Can be applied thickly to leather-hard or bisque ware.

Many of the above base glazes can be coloured with the addition of the following oxides.

Cobalt Carbonate	0.5 per cent produces medium blue
Cobalt Carbonate	1 per cent produces strong blue
Copper Carbonate	2 per cent produces light green
Copper Carbonate	4 per cent produces strong green

Iron Oxide	2 per cent produces tan
Iron Oxide	4 per cent produces medium brown
Iron Oxide	6 per cent produces dark brown
Manganese Carbonate	4 per cent produces medium purple
Manganese Carbonate	6 per cent produces dark purple
Chrome Oxide	2 per cent produces green
Rutileh	5 per cent produces tan
Nickel Oxide	2 per cent produces grey or brown
Vanadium Stain	6 per cent produces medium yellow

Cobalt Carbonate 0.5 per cent + Iron Oxide 2 per cent	grey blue
Cobalt Carbonate 0.5 per cent + Manganese Dioxide 5 per cent	purple blue
Cobalt Carbonate 0.5 per cent + Copper Carbonate 2 per cent	blue green
Copper Carbonate 2 per cent + Iron Oxide 2 per cent	warm yellow
Copper Carbonate 3 per cent + Vanadium Stain 3 per cent	warm green
Cobalt Carbonate 0.5 per cent + Rutile 3 per cent	warm blue
Vanadium Stain 5 per cent + Rutile 4 per cent	warm ochre

Stoneware Glaze Recipes

The use of dry stoneware glazes allows you to produce a wider range of colours and surface qualities.

PETER PHILLIP'S SLIP GLAZE 1280°C
REDUCTION

China Clay	45
Whiting	45
Borax Frit	10
Ball Clay	10

This base glaze will give a variety of colours (breaking rust red where thin) depending on what oxides are added. 0.5–1 per cent Cobalt Oxide will give blues. 1–2 per cent Iron Oxide will give yellow/ochre colours. Copper and Rutile are also worth trying.

MEDWAY BARIUM BLUE 1280°C
REDUCTION

Barium Carbonate	33.5
Nepheline Syenite	50
China Clay	16.9
Copper Carbonate	3

A dry turquoise blue that also works well over decoration in a strong blue slip.

SIDDIG EL'NIGOUMI'S MATT
BLUE/GREEN GLAZE 1250–1300°C
REDUCTION

Potash Feldspar	40
China Clay	38
Whiting	20
Cobalt Oxide	1
Red Iron Oxide	1

This glaze responds very well to double dipping.

Ungrogged Bodies

SRB 8 supplied by
Spencroft Ceramics

SANDED BODY supplied by
Valentine Clay Products

WCM 52 (powdered body)
Alpha Whitfield

Sanded Bodies

EVANS BODY supplied by Spencroft
Ceramics

SANDED BODY supplied by Valentine
Clay Products

REAL TERRACOTTA (A highly plastic
locally dug body) supplied by Ruaradene
Pottery

*WHITE EARTHENWARE BODIES
WHITE EARTHENWARE CLAY*
supplied by Spencroft Ceramics

Stoneware Bodies

HT STONEWARE
Craft Crank mixed together 50/50.
Both clays are supplied by
Valentine Clay Products

ST THOMAS REDUCTION
Craft Crank mixed together 50/50.
Both clays are supplied by
Potclays Ltd

8 Setting Up and Running Your Business

Marketing and Selling

Small businesses and sole traders often grossly underestimate the importance of this activity. It really does not matter how good your product is, in terms of quality and value, if it's not put under the noses of the people who are likely to buy it. Hand-crafted products by their nature are more labour-intensive to produce than machine-made objects and therefore must command a higher price. Many members of the public fail to recognize this, which unfortunately means we are operating in somewhat of a niche market. There are some very good books on both marketing and in a wider sense setting up and running a business that I strongly advise you to read if you lack experience in these areas. My own experience before running a business was exclusively limited to making pots, and in an arrogant sort of way I just assumed that people would be falling over themselves to buy them. Strangely enough though most people did not seem to share my passion for hand-made terracotta pots and I soon realized that I was going to have to acquire some new skills pretty quickly if I was going to be able to make my own living. In this section all I really want to do is share some of my experiences and the lessons I've learnt along the way.

Marketing

What does this term really mean? Well it is an umbrella term that covers everything from research, product planning and development to promotion and of course selling. I will try to keep it fairly simple though and see in practical terms what each one means to us as potters.

Research, product planning and development. Before you start to develop your range of pots be sure to check out your competitors. There are some excellent British Terracotta makers. Go to their workshops as a customer, have a good look around and buy their catalogues to see what range they are making and what their pricing structure is. This will give you a very good overview of their business, and what you will be competing against. Visit some of the more exclusive garden centres, ones that are likely to stock high-quality terracotta. Not only will this give you a good indication of what is currently selling

The author outside his workshop.

but also whether it's worth approaching them at a later date to stock your pots. Try to attend some of the premier Garden Shows such as Chelsea Flower Show and Hampton Court Flower Show. You may make some good contacts and it will give you the best indication of current fashions. In the late 1990s for instance the sale of terracotta pots seems to be dwindling, after having sold very well for fifteen years or more, with companies such as Whichford Pottery and Willow Pottery making their names by producing them. Now though it seems that it's time for a change with many companies starting to produce brightly coloured pots, many of which are made of Buff clay. If your business is to be successful it is very important to keep up with these trends and whenever possible to be one step ahead.

Promotion. This can be broken down into the following areas: business cards and leaflets, catalogues, public shows, trade fairs and the workshop. When dealing with clients and potential clients, members of the general public or business community, it is absolutely vital to be totally professional. One way of helping to achieve this is to have professional literature. Business cards and leaflets are a fairly cheap way of making yourself look established and serious about what you are doing. Generally people do not remember your name or even your company name but they will remember the most striking feature of your work. When choosing an image it is often best to avoid using a group shot of pots, because when you change your range it may make your literature out of date. Instead choose a feature which is instantly recognizable as your work but slightly more abstract such as a swag or style of decoration.

I have found catalogues to be an extremely useful way of promoting my work. It is not essential to produce them with full-colour glossy images but do the best you can with the budget you have. If you are selling at public fairs or by mail order you may decide to invest a considerable amount into a catalogue and have one professionally printed. In these circumstances it would not be unreasonable to charge the general public a small fee to purchase it, although you would generally supply to the trade for free. My first catalogue consisted of a series of line drawings of each pot I made, each drawing was accompanied by the range of sizes it was available in and a reference number so it could be identified easily. These were photocopied onto coloured paper then stapled together to form a small booklet. Although this was fairly crude and it is possible to do much better now on a home computer, it served its purpose well, with many sales resulting from it. The one word of warning I have to offer is that it's not uncommon to chop and change pots in the first few months after setting up. It is best to establish your range first and find out what sells well for you before going ahead and producing your catalogue. You will want to get at least two years' use from it before it needs replacing. Price lists are generally printed on separate sheets so the same catalogues can be distributed to both trade and retail customers. It also allows you to adjust your prices from time to time without having to reprint your catalogue.

Public shows and trade fairs. These will be dealt with in greater depth in the following section on selling but it is important not to forget their value in terms of promoting your business. At many of these events thousands of people will pass by your stand but practically no one will buy anything. This may be for a number of reasons – maybe it's simply because they just do not want your product, in which case you are very unlikely to ever get a sale from them. However there are many other reasons why they may not buy from you on a particular occasion. Maybe they are not looking for flower pots at that time but will be at a later date, perhaps they have made too many purchases before reaching you and have no money left. It could simply be that terracotta pots are very heavy and they can't get them home easily. The best approach is to treat everyone as a potential future customer, be polite, friendly and give away as many business cards or leaflets as possible. Sometimes what may appear a poor show in terms of sales on the day may prove worthwhile after all, even if it brings in only one good customer. If you have visitors to your workshop on a regular basis the same principle applies, it is worth making the effort to be friendly, polite and take time to explain what you are making and how you are doing it. This seems obvious but it's easy to lose sight of when you are feeling pressurized by uncompleted orders and you've been asked 'where does your clay come from?' for the tenth time that morning. Even if they do not buy anything, if they have enjoyed their visit they will tell their friends who may well come and buy.

Selling

There are two options open to you; either selling directly to the trade (wholesale) or to the general public (retail) and a different approach is required for each.

SELLING DIRECTLY TO THE PUBLIC

Selling to the public can be subdivided into selling at Craft Fairs, Garden Shows or directly from the workshop. The most profitable way is to sell directly from the workshop as it avoids the considerable costs involved with exhibiting at a fair and the time taken to set up, run and dismantle a stand. It is a consideration that should be borne in mind when choosing the sight for your workshop. Many major tourist attractions for instance, are very happy to rent space to crafts people fairly cheaply in exchange for you doing regular demonstrations for their visitors. If you are fortunate enough to have the opportunity to rent a workshop on one of these sites, be aware of the pitfalls. Be sure to keep exclusive rights for the sale of your work – if they want to stock your work in their gift shop for instance, they should buy it at trade price. Secondly, be careful over contractual obligations concerning your opening times. They may try to commit you to being open all the hours they are, resulting in you having to work a seven-day week, or pay someone to cover you if you want time off. This can also make taking time off to participate in craft fairs and garden shows awkward. One possible solution to this problem is to find another craftsperson to share the workshop with you. This will reduce both the time you are obligated to spend there and the overheads such as rent and business rates.

Public Fairs and Garden Shows can be a very worthwhile way of selling your work. Many crafts people make their living exclusively from selling at these events. Until you have personal experience of which organizers and shows work for you though, be very wary of committing yourself to a series of them, particularly with just one organizer. It can be a minefield, at some fairs (particularly the smaller ones) you may not even sell enough pots to cover the cost of your pitch, not to mention your time that is lost from production. Bear in mind that a weekend show will often take you away from production for a whole week. The shows may run for three days, (especially on a bank holiday weekend) with the two days prior to the show spent boxing and packing the pots, travelling to the show and setting up the stand. The day following the show is spent travelling home and unpacking. I have been in the unpleasant situation of making a loss at a show a number of times and remember thinking that I would have been no worse off if I had stayed at home and given the few pots I had sold away over the garden fence. This would have avoided the stall fee and petrol costs and would have given me a rare few days at home in the garden. Don't be put off though, just be warned – if you are seriously considering selling on the craft/garden fair circuit, it can be very rewarding with the proper research. Read the following points very carefully – the advice given therein was learnt at great financial cost and with considerable pain attached.

Try to get literature from as many organizers as possible before you book any shows (there are some listed in a later section). Be aware that they are selling a product, namely their show, and will make it sound very appealing. Try not to be too taken in by this, and isolate the facts, there are several key points you will need to satisfy prior to booking. How long have they been established? Be wary of organizers that have been established for less than two years. How long has the show you are inquiring about been run at that venue? If it's been running for several years (maybe five or six) it is more likely to be successful. What are the average attendance figures for their shows? Get the breakdown for individual shows, a good one will expect around ten thousand people. Are there any other crafts people exhibiting similar products to you? Most shows (unless they are very large) will not be able to support more than two stalls exhibiting the same product range. What is the entrance fee to the public and does it seem good value for money? A high entrance fee may possibly have some impact on your customers' spend-

ing power. Lastly and most importantly, what is the size and price of a pitch? Don't forget to include hidden extras such as parking, camping, electricity, lighting, tables, chairs and VAT. From this you can work out the exact price of your stand. Bear in mind that for a show to be successful it will need to turnover three to four times its cost.

Wherever possible, visit the show as a member of the public before booking it (sometimes complimentary tickets are available if you ring the organizers and say you are considering booking). Ask yourself, is it well advertised and signposted? Does it seem busy? Ask the stallholders (particularly those with a similar type of product and price range to you) how they are finding the show and the organizers, and whether they have attended the show before or intend to again. Most are quite helpful if you tell them you are thinking of exhibiting yourself.

The last word of warning comes purely from personal experience. Avoid small-scale, cheap organizers like the plague. I'm sure this approach is very prejudiced as there are bound to be some good small-scale organizers somewhere, but it is borne out of bitter experience. An unsuccessful show leaves you feeling totally demoralized, sometimes even questioning whether or not it might be time for a change of career. Small events never seem properly organized, advertised or attended and you can guarantee that there will be a hobby potter on the next but one stall selling their work for next to nothing. Their priority being to clear valuable space from their small work areas, not making a living. In fact the only stalls that do seem to do quite well at these events are the cake and fudge stands, a phenomenon that I have always found a little curious, even ironic. Why is it that crafts people who are passionate about their chosen profession and spend years sometimes learning their craft, and honing their skills, often struggle to make a living? While the fudge makers who need only limited equipment, a few pre-packed ingredients and a short instruction pamphlet sell their 'wares' in huge amounts?

I hope it doesn't seem as though I am bitter about my craft fair experiences because on the whole it's quite the contrary. Generally I have found shows profitable and tremendous fun to take part in, there is always an air of expectation and excitement before a good show. Once you have been on the circuit for a while you will soon be welcomed into the 'community' that is by and large very friendly. My only really bad experiences came in the first few months after setting up, exhibiting at small fairs. As soon as I turned to the more 'professional' craft fair circuit my sales (and profits) increased dramatically. This was accomplished without making any alterations to my product range.

All of the above information is also applicable to garden shows, the one obvious difference being you can guarantee that all of the attending public will have an interest in the garden. Before you jump for joy and race out to book the next available show, remember that all of your competitors will be selling garden related products too. Instead of competing against one or two other stalls as is normal at a craft fair, you will be competing with every stall. This is not a problem as long as you aware of this fact, so try to be creative when designing your range of pots and offer the public something original, a range of work that will set you apart from the rest.

SELLING TO THE TRADE

You basically have three alternatives, selling at trade fairs (which we have covered already) cold calling or by making an appointment to see a buyer. The approach should be the same whichever method you choose, be thoroughly prepared, totally organized and very professional. Cold calling can work very well particularly for small outlets such as plant nurseries and small shops, but be careful not to be a nuisance. Under no circumstances should you march into a busy store, drop your box of pots on the counter and demand to see the manager! Choose a quiet morning to introduce yourself to the manager/owner and explain what you make. If they are not too busy it may then be possible to show them some samples; if it is inconvenient it may be possible to arrange an appointment for another time. For larger outlets such as department stores and large garden centres you will almost certainly have to contact the buyer and make an appointment. Large stores may well have a buyer for each department, whose name may be obtained easily by ringing the store directly. Many will expect you to send samples or catalogues before they will agree to see you.

When showing your work to a potential customer, whether it's Harrods or the local nursery around the corner, I can't stress enough how important is it to be thoroughly prepared. Try to avoid using newspaper to pack your pots, it doesn't look very professional and it tends to go everywhere when you unpack them. Bubble wrap or similar packing material is a much better option. When you pack the pots, be sure you know the position of each one in the box and work out some logical order in which to show them. Point out which pots are your best-sellers or which ones you think would be most suitable for them. It often helps to stick labels to the bases of the pots with a reference number and a trade price on. Even if you are sure you know the prices, they can go out of your head in the middle of a meeting when the pressure is on. If you intend to offer free delivery it is quite normal, in fact almost expected that you will have a price set for a minimum order. If this proves to be a problem and you think it may cost you an order you can always make a concession if you want (this will make your new customer think they are getting special treatment). When you take the order, be very clear about the delivery date and method of payment. Do not be unrealistic about how long orders take to make (it is nearly always longer than you imagine). Shops are generally prepared to wait if you are honest in the first place but if they feel that they are being given the runaround it may cost you a repeat order. Cash on delivery is the preferred method of payment but many trade customers will expect to pay on account with thirty days being a normal time scale. Large department stores often have their own system, which involves setting up a special account and you will often have to accept payment on their terms.

Business Paperwork

If you have never written a receipt or invoice before then tackling the associated paperwork may seem a little daunting. There is a set business standard to follow though, and it is fairly simple once you are in the swing of it. All documentation should be made in duplicate, one copy for your records and one for your customers. It is worth buying separate duplicate books with pre-printed headings for orders, invoices and receipts – they will need to be referred to when completing your books and this will make accessing the information more straightforward.

Order Form

This is just a simple record of what your customer has ordered (including reference numbers if you have them) the total price and date of delivery. This doesn't have to be too specific – a number of weeks is adequate.

```
ORDER FORM

Your Business Name  _____      Date  _____
Address and Tel:    _____
                    _____
                    _____

Your Customer's Name  _____
Address and Tel:      _____
                      _____
                      _____

DETAILS OF THE ORDER  _____
DATE OF DELIVERY      _____
                      _____
TOTAL PRICE           _____
```

Delivery Note

This is used as a record of what you have delivered, is sent with the order and should be signed by your customer to prove that the order arrived complete and undamaged. If you are delivering the order yourself and your customer is making payment on delivery then this can be dispensed with.

DELIVERY NOTE

Your Business Name _____   Date _____

Address and Tel: _____

_____

_____

Your Customer's Name _____

Address and Tel: _____

_____

_____

DETAILS OF THE ORDER _____

SIGNED BY YOUR CUSTOMER _____

Invoice

The invoice is used to let your customer know that you would like to receive payment for the pots you have supplied them with. If your customer is making payment on delivery they can be issued with a receipt and this can be dispensed with.

INVOICE

Your Business Name _____   Date _____

Address and Tel: _____

_____

_____

Your Customer's Name _____

Address and Tel: _____

_____

_____

DETAILS OF THE ORDER _____

PAYMENT DUE _____

Statement

This is used to remind customers who are paying on account that payment is due immediately. It should be sent just before the period of payment expires. If payment is still not received within a reasonable period then it is often best to pursue it over the telephone or in person. The format is exactly the same as that for the invoice.

Receipt

Once payment has been received most customers will require a receipt. This is very simple and can even be dispensed with if you: sign, date and write PAID IN FULL on the invoice. It is worth making a note of the method of payment too, such as cash or cheque (write down the cheque number); when doing your books it makes cross-referencing much easier.

RECEIPT

Your Business Name _____   Date _____
Address and Tel: _____
                  _____
                  _____

Your Customer's Name _____
Address and Tel: _____
                     _____
                     _____

DETAILS OF THE ORDER _____

RECEIVED WITH THANKS (The amount and method of payment)
_____

SIGNED BY YOURSELF _____

Costing and Pricing

Very often potters arrive at prices for their pots without properly costing them, preferring instead to rely on experience, they base their prices in relation to other pots they produce, or on what the 'going rate' may be for a particular pot. Serious consideration should be paid to these conclusions. I know from personal experience there is a ceiling to the price I can charge for my pots. If I set the price beyond that rate, sales often fall off dramatically. However, it is not wise to base prices on this information alone.

The results of a costing exercise will give you a good indication of the profit margins for a particular pot. It takes into account the Fixed Costs such as rent and rates, the Variable Costs such as materials and firings and the Labour Costs. Therefore it will also give you a clear picture of what your time and money is spent on, vital information if you are running your own business. If your profit margins are small you will inevitably end up working very long hours maybe sixty or even eighty per week. A full and thorough costing exercise will enable you to identify those pots that are non-profitable and adjust them accordingly, by either: raising the price of the pot, finding a quicker method of production or making more profitable pots instead.

A Costing Exercise

It is easiest to break the costs down into fixed costs, variable costs and labour costs, then work them out separately; the results are then collated to arrive at a price.

Labour Costs

When working out labour costs it is all too easy to forget non-production-related tasks such as kiln packing, tidying and deliveries and arrive at a price by simply thinking, 'I can throw that pot in "X" minutes so therefore the price is £X'. For this reason timesheets need to be drawn up and filled in over a fairly extended period (two weeks should be a bare minimum with a whole month being much better). Your every movement needs to be accounted for and catalogued to give you a clear picture of how much time you spend on the production-related tasks and the non-production-related tasks. Assuming you work a 40-hour week the results for two weeks' survey may look something like this:

N.B. Although strictly speaking kiln packing is a production-related task, this costing exercise calculates a price for a pot by knowing what percentage of your time is spent preparing clay, throwing, decorating and glazing a single pot.

Production-Related Tasks (PRT)			Non-Production-Related Tasks (NPRT)		
Clay Preparation	12hr 50min	(12.8)	Kiln Packing	8 hr	(8)
Throwing	26hr 25min	(26.4)	Tidying	3hr 10min	(3.2)
Decorating	15hr 10min	(15.2)	Deliveries	4hr 50min	(4.8)
Glazing	2hr 25min	(2.4)	Phone Calls and Paperwork		
			(inc. Marketing)	6hr 25min	(6.4)

The objective is to express the above timings as a percentage. To do this the hours and minutes need to be converted into a decimal format which can be done quite simply by dividing the total minutes by sixty.

E.g. Clay preparation 12hr 50min becomes 12.8 (50min) (50min = 0.8 hr)

The figures are now converted into percentages by dividing the time for an individual task (clay preparation 12.8) by the total hours worked (80), this is then multiplied by 100 (total 16 per cent).

Expressed as a formula it looks like this:

$$\frac{\text{Time spent on individual task}}{\text{Total Hours worked}} \times 100$$

$$\frac{12.8}{80} \times 100 = 16 \text{ per cent}$$

Production-Related Tasks (PRT)	%	Non Production Related Tasks (NPRT)	%
Clay preparation	16	Kiln packing	10
Throwing	33	Tidying	4
Decorating	19	Deliveries	6
Glazing	3	Phone calls and paperwork (including marketing)	8
TOTAL	71		
		TOTAL	71

When expressed as a percentage, these figures can often be quite revealing. Even after twelve years of potting it is a constant surprise to me how little time I apparently spend on the wheel, throwing.

Once these percentages have been calculated you can relate them to any pot you produce. They will only need to be recalculated if your working practices change. Choose the pot you want to work a price out for, make a batch of them (enough to last you at least a couple of hours) and time the individual processes. It may be as follows:

Making 30 × 4lb flowerpots
Preparation time	46 minutes
Throwing time	1 hour 50 minutes (110 minutes)
Decorating time	36 minutes

Total production time is   46 + 110 + 36 = 192 minutes

N.B. The pot chosen is unglazed, for glazed pots include a timing for this operation.

In 192 minutes 30 flowerpots were produced. From this result we can very easily work out how long it takes to produce one flowerpot.

$$\frac{\text{Number of pots produced}}{\text{Time taken to produce pots}} \quad \frac{30}{192} = \text{Time taken to produce one pot } 6.4$$

Or

$$192 \div 30 = 6.4 \text{ minutes per pot}$$

We can see from our earlier percentages for production-related tasks that the processes we timed when producing these pots (preparation, throwing and decorating) only account for 68 per cent of the total time spent at work. Therefore 6.4 minutes per pot is not a true average time as it does not include any time for non-production related tasks. A more accurate average timing can be worked out by calculating 68 per cent of 30 pots.

This is 30 pots × 68 per cent (PRT) = 20.4 pots in 192 minutes

The length of time needed to produce one pot is calculated by:

192 minutes ÷ 20.4 pots = 9.4 minutes per pot

With this figure it is possible to calculate how many pots can be produced on average in an hour, day or week, essential information to know when taking on large orders. The amount of pots produced in a week is worked out as follows:

(Total minutes in 1 week) 2,400 minutes ÷ 9.4 = 255.3 pots per week

For the purpose of this costing exercise though, we need to know how many pots can be made in one hour, this is:

Total minutes in one hour (60 minutes) 9.4min per pot = 6.3 pots per hour

The labour cost for an individual pot is worked out by dividing your hourly rate by the number of pots you can make in one hour.

Where the hourly rate is £10 the labour cost of one pot is:

£10 ÷ 6.3pots per hour = £1.59

Total Labour costs for one pot = £1.59

Fixed Overheads
Any payments you make that are not affected by the volume of pots you produce such as rent, rates, loans, exhibition fees and vehicle costs are included in this section. The fixed overheads can be worked out simply by totalling them for one week and dividing them by the number of hours worked in one week. For example:

Rent	£35
Loans	£20
Business rates	£35
Exhibition fees	£18
Vehicle costs	£22

Total cost of fixed overheads per week £130

When the fixed cost for the workshop are £130 per week the cost for one hour is:

130 total overheads (40hours per week = £3.25)

Total fixed costs £3.25 per hour

From this figure we can calculate the fixed costs for one pot, which is:

The cost per hour divided by the number of pots that can be made in one hour.

£3.25 Total fixed costs per hour ÷ 6.3 number of pots made in 1 hour = 51p

Total fixed costs for one pot = 51p

Variable Costs
All costs, which vary depending on the amount of pots you make such as material costs (clay and glaze) and firing costs (gas and electric), are included in this section. Clay costs can be worked out quite simply by dividing the price of one bag, by the weight of the bag, then, multiplying this figure by the weight of the pot. For example:

Where the weight of one bag of clay is 56lb (or 25kg), the cost is £5.00 and the weight of the pot is 4lb, it is:

£5.00 ÷ 56lb = 8 pence per 1lb of clay
4lb × 8p = 32p

Total clay costs for the pot = 32p

Oxides, frits and certain other glaze materials can be very expensive to buy so it is important to have some way of calculating the cost for glaze on an individual pot. One way of doing this is to work out the cost for the whole bucket of glaze then measure the depth of glaze in the bucket. Next dip a batch of pots and re-measure the depth of glaze in the bucket. From this measurement the percentage of the glaze that has been used can be calculated, this figure is then divided by the number of pots in the batch that were dipped.

The firing cost can be worked out simply by dividing the cost of one firing by the amount of pots that will fit into the kiln. For instance :

£12 per firing ÷30 pots = total firing costs for one pot = 40p)

We now have all of the individual results necessary to calculate the exact cost of producing one pot. By simply adding them together we will arrive at the result.

Labour costs	£1.59
Fixed costs	£0.51
Clay costs	£0.32
Firing costs	£0.40
TOTAL	£2.82

The total cost of producing one pot is £2.82

The above figure is the cost of producing a 4lb flowerpot, excluding any charge for profit. A percentage will need to be added to allow you to reinvest funds into your business. The exact amount should be a personal decision based on the state of the market – that is, if your goods are in demand then your profit margins can be high.

$\mathscr{9}$ Useful Formulae

Brongniart's Formula

Alexander Brongniart, the director of the Sèvres porcelain factory in the early part of the nineteenth-century, is perhaps best known to studio potters for his formula for finding the dry weight of a suspended solid in a slip. It is used when drying out a material will be too time consuming – so in practical terms if a material has been ball milled or when you wish to add sand, grog or barium carbonate for instance to a blunged body. It is worked out by an algebraic calculation but the principles are as follows.

$$\text{DRY WEIGHT} = \text{APPARENT DRY WEIGHT} \times \frac{\text{SPECIFIC GRAVITY}}{\text{SPECIFIC GRAVITY} - 1}$$

Apparent dry weight is the weight of one pint of slip, minus the weight of one pint of water. The weight of one pint of a fluid is known as pint weight and for water it is 20oz. Apparent dry weight should not be confused with true dry weight, which is related to the specific gravity of a material. Specific gravity is the number of times a substance is heavier than water. It is expressed as a number and China Clay for example is 2.5. Other materials are listed later.

W is dry weight required; P is pint weight; SG is specific gravity.

The formula is as follows.

$$W = (P - 20) \times \frac{SG}{SG - 1}$$

For example, a China Clay slip would be worked out as follows.

Pint weight = 28oz
Specific gravity = 2.5

$$W = (28 - 20) \times \frac{2.5}{(2.5 - 1)}$$

$$W = 8 \times \frac{2.5}{1.5}$$

$$W = 8 \times 1.666$$

$$W = 13.328$$

The dry weight of 1 pint of China Clay slip is 13.3oz

Therefore one gallon would weigh $8 \times 13.3 = 106.4$oz or 6.6lb

Many potters still work in imperial measurements but for those who prefer metric the formula is expressed as follows.

$$\text{DRY WEIGHT} = (\text{SLIP WEIGHT} - 100) \times \frac{SG}{SG-1}$$

Where 100cc of water weigh 100g, slip weight is the weight of 100cc of slip.

Converting Temperatures

Most firing temperatures are given in centigrade but for those occasions when you encounter Fahrenheit measurements, the conversion is as follows.

$$°C = \frac{(°F - 32 \times 5)}{9}$$

Or should you wish to convert to Fahrenheit

$$°F = \left(°C \times \frac{9}{5}\right) + 32$$

Conversion of Dry Weights

Ounces to grams	$\times 28.35$
Pounds to kilograms	$\times 0.4536$
Grams to ounces	$\times 0.0353$
Kilograms to pounds	$\times 2.2046$

Specific Gravity

When working out the dry weight of a slip it is necessary to know the specific gravities of the material you are using when it is dry. Clay should be taken to be 2.5 while other materials are listed below.

Specific Gravities of Common Materials		
MATERIAL	CHEMICAL FORMULA	SPECIFIC GRAVITY
Barium Carbonate	$BaCO_3$	4.4
Bone Ash	$Ca_3(PO_4)_2$	3.1
China Clay	$Al_2O_3 . 2SiO_2 . 2H_2O$	2.5
Cobalt Carbonate	$CoCO_3$	4.0
Cobalt Oxide	CoO_4	5.7
Copper Carbonate	$CuCO_3$	5.0
Copper Oxide	CuO	6.4
Flint	SiO_2	2.6
Iron Oxide (red)	Fe_2O_3	5.3
Iron Oxide (black)	FeO	5.7
Potash Feldspar	$K_2O . Al_2O_3 . 6SiO_2$	2.6
Lead Bisilicate	$PbO . 2SiO_2$	4.5
Manganese Dioxide	MnO_2	4.9
Nepheline Syenite	$K_2O . 3NaO_2 . 4Al_2O_3 . 9SiO_2$	2.6
Nickel Oxide	NiO	6.7
Quartz	SiO_2	2.7
Rutile	TiO_2	4.2
Talc	$3MgO . 4SiO_2 . 2H_2O$	2.7
Tin Oxide	SnO_2	6.8
Titanium Dioxide	TiO_2	4.2
Whiting	$CaCO_3$	2.8
Wollastonite	$CaSiO_3$	2.8
Yellow Ochre	$2Fe_2O_3 . 3H_2O$	3.5
Zinc Oxide	ZnO	5.7
Zirconium Silicate	$ZrSiO_4$	4.5

Useful Addresses

Craft Fair and Garden Show Organizers

Garden Shows

RHS Shows Department
80 Vincent Square
London
SW1P 2PE
Tel: 0171 630 7422
Fax: 0171 233 9525

The RHS organizes many shows including the Chelsea Flower Show, Hampton Court Flower Show, The Malvern Spring Garden Show and Scotland's National Garden Show. All RHS shows are very well organized. It is important to apply early (in some cases even nine months in advance).

Grow, The Garden Experience
Protech Promotions Ltd
Grenfell House
Grenfell Avenue
Hornchurch
Essex
RM12 4DN
Tel: 01708 455907
Fax: 01708 455908

Romor Exhibitions Limited
Garden Shows
PO Box 448
Bedford
MK40 2ZP
Tel: 01234 345725
Fax: 01234 328604

The National Amateur Gardening Show
Sovereign Exhibition Management
Bramley House
Combe Wood
Coombe Street
Nicholas
Chard
Somerset
TA20 3NN
Tel: 01460 66616
Fax : 01460 66636

Craft Fairs

The British Craft Trade Fair (at Harrogate and London)
Marathon Events Management Limited
The All England Jumping Course
London Road
Hickstead
W. Sussex RH17 5NX
Tel: 01273 833884

Craft Movement
PO Box 1641
Frome
Somerset
BA11 1YY
Tel: 01373 813333

The Ideal Home Exhibition
Times House
Station Approach
Ruislip
Middlesex
HA4 8NB
Tel: 01895 677677
Fax: 01895 625740

Rainbow Fairs
Navigation Wharf
Carre Street
Sleaford
Lincs
NG34 7TW
Tel: 01529 414793

The Daily Telegraph/
House & Garden Fair
National Events Ltd
Francis House
King's Head Yard
London
SE1 1NA
Tel: 0171 453 5326
Fax: 0171 453 5305

ICHF
Dominic House
Seaton Road
Highcliffe
Dorset
BH23 5HW
Tel: 01425 272711
Fax: 01425 279369

Pottery Suppliers

Acme Marls Ltd
Bournes Bank
Burslem
Stoke-on-Trent
Staffs
ST6 3DW
Tel: 01782 577757
Fax: 01782 575368

Aeromatic Barter Ltd
Kynock Road
Ely East
Edmonton
London
N18 3BH
Tel: 0181 803 8302

Alpha Whitfield
Whitfield House
10 Water Street
Newcastle-under-Lyme
Staffs
ST5 1HP
Tel: 01782 711155
Fax: 01782 712510

Arnold, J. & Sons Ltd
Billington Road
Leighton Buzzard
Beds

Bates Electrical
67 Bournes Bank
Burslem
Stoke-on-Trent
ST6 3DP
Tel/Fax: 01782 837939

Branham, C.H. & Co Ltd
Roundswell Industrial
   Estate
Stickle Path
Barnstaple
Devon
Tel: 01271 376853

Bricesco Ltd
Rowhurst Industrial Estate
Rowhurst Close
Chesterton
Newcastle-Under-Lyme
Staffs
ST5 6BH
Tel: 01782 566921
Fax: 01782 562792

British Ceramic Research
(CERAM Research)
Queens Road
Penkill
Stoke-on-Trent
Staffs
ST4 7LQ
Tel: 01782 845431
Fax: 01782 412331

British Gypsum Ltd
Industrial Products
   Division
Jericho Works
Bowbridge Lane
Newark
Notts
NG24 3BZ
Tel: 01636 703351
Fax: 01636 673542

Central Ceramic Services
Ltd
Cartwright Industrial
   Estate
Spring Garden Road
Longton
Stoke-on-Trent
Staffs
ST3 2TE
Tel: 01782 598400
Fax: 01782 598098

Ceramic Product
Development
Cinderhill Industrial
   Estate
Weston Coyney Road
Longton
Stoke-on-Trent
Staffs
ST3 5JU
Tel: 01782 599290
Fax 01782 596325

*Cookson Matthey Ceramics
& Materials Ltd*
Uttoxeter Road
Meir
Stoke-on-Trent
Staffs
ST3 7XW
Tel: 01782 599111
Fax: 01782 337127

Cromartie Kilns Ltd
Park Hall Road
Longton
Stoke-on-Trent
Staffs
ST3 5AY
Tel: 01782 313947
Fax: 01782 599723

CTM Supplies
9 Spruce Close
Exeter
EX4 9JU
Tel/Fax: 01392 464384

Diamond Gimson
King Street
Fenton
Stoke-on-Trent
Staffs
ST4 3LY
Tel: 01782 744821
Fax: 01782 747200

Drayton Kilns Ltd
Plantation Road
Newstead Trading Estate
Trenham
Stoke-on-Trent
Staffs
ST4 8HX
Tel: 01782 657361
Fax: 01782 658946

ECC International Europe
John Keay House
St Austell
Cornwall
PL25 4DJ
Tel: 01726 623598
Fax: 01726 623019

Edward & Jones Ltd
Whittle Road
Meir
Stoke-on-Trent
ST3 7QD
Tel: 01782 599000
Fax: 01782 599001

Fast Fire Ltd
Unit 23, Britannia Park
   Industrial Estate
North Road
Cobridge
Stoke-on-Trent
Staffs
ST6 2PZ

Hand, J.W. & Partners
Greendock Street
Longton
Stoke-on-Trent
ST3 2NZ
Tel: 01782 311452
Fax: 01782 599513

Johnson Tiles H&R
Highgate Tile Works
Brown Hills Road
Tunstall
Stoke-on-Trent
Staffs
ST6 4JX
Tel: 01782 575575

Kilns & Furnaces
Keele Street
Tunstall
Stoke-on-Trent
Staffs
Tel: 01782 813621
Fax: 01782 575379

Laser Kilns Ltd
Unit 9
Crispin Industrial Centre
Angel Road Works
London
N18 2DT
Tel: 0181 803 1016
Fax: 0181 807 2888

The Milliput Company
Unit 5
The Marian
Dolgellau
Gwynedd
Mid Wales
LL40 1UU
Tel/Fax: 01341 422562

Potclays Ltd
Brickkiln Lane
Etruria
Stoke-on-Trent
Tel: 01782 219816

Pottery Crafts
Campbell Road
Stoke-on-Trent
Staffs
ST4 4ET
Tel: 01782 745000
Fax: 01782 746000

*Ratcliffe, J.W. & Sons
(Engineering) Ltd*
Rope Works
Rope Street, off Shelton
   New Road
Stoke-on-Trent
Tel: 01782 717300
Fax: 01782 717136

Rayefco Ltd
Lomnfield
Bulstrode Lane
Feldon
Hemel Hempstead
Herts
HP3 0BP
Tel/Fax 01442 242332

Spencroft Ceramics
Spencroft Road
Holditch Industrial Estate
Newcastle-under-Lyme
Staffs
Tel: 01782 627004

Stokes, D.J.E.
Haulage Contractor
56 Doxey Fields
Stafford
Tel: 01785 254715

Valentine Clay Products
The Sliphouse
Birches Head Road
Hanley
Stoke-on-Trent
Staffs
ST4 2SP
Tel: 01782 627004
Fax: 01782

Watts Blake Bearne & Co PLC
Park House
Courtenay Park
Newton Abbot
Devon
TQ12 4PS
Tel: 01626 332345
Fax: 01626 332344

Whitfield & Sons Ltd
Lakeside
Festival Way
Festival Park
Stoke-on-Trent
Tel: 01782 219933

General Pottery Suppliers

Supplying clay bodies, raw materials and equipment.

Potclays Ltd
Pottery Crafts

Materials

CLAY SUPPLIERS

Alpha Whitfield
Cookson Matthey
ECC International Europe
Potclays Ltd
Pottery Crafts
Watts Blake Bearne & Co.
Whitfield & Sons Ltd.

PLASTIC BODIES

Branham, C.H. & Co Ltd
Potclays
Pottery Crafts
Spencroft Ceramics
Valentine Clay Products.

CASTING SLIP

Potclays Ltd
Pottery Crafts
Valentine Clay Products.

RAW MATERIALS

Alpha Whitfield
Cookson Matthey
CTM Supplies
Potclays Ltd
Pottery Crafts
Whitfield & Sons Ltd.

SAND

Arnold, J. & Sons Ltd.

PLASTER

Alpha Whitfield
British Gypsum
Potclays Ltd
Pottery Crafts.

Equipment

KILN SUPPLIERS

Cromartie Kilns Ltd
Drayton Kilns Ltd
Fast Fire Ltd
Kilns & Furnaces
Potclays Ltd
Pottery Crafts.

KILN FIBRE

Whitfield & Sons Ltd.

KILN FURNITURE

Acme Marls Ltd
Diamond Gimson
Potclays Ltd
Pottery Crafts.

KILN BURNERS

Aeromatic Barter Ltd
Bricesco Ltd.

POTTER'S WHEELS

Potclays Ltd
Pottery Crafts
Ratcliffe, J.W. & Sons
(Engineering) Ltd
Rayefco Ltd (wheels for sale
and hire).

FILTER PRESSES

Ratcliffe, J.W. & Sons
(Engineering) Ltd
Edwards & Jones.

PUGMILLS

Potclays Ltd
Pottery Crafts.

PUMPS

Central Ceramic Services.
Edward & Jones

PLASTER MOULDS (BLOCK, CASE AND WORKING)

Ceramic Product
Development
Hand, J.W. & Partners.

TESTING AND RESEARCH

British Ceramic Research.

FILLER (FOR POT REPAIRS)

The Milliput Company.

BISQUE THROWING TILES

Johnson Tiles H&R.

Haulage

Stokes, D.J.E.

Index